OXFORD REVISION GUIDES

AS & A Level

PHYSICAL EDUCATION

through diagrams

David Morton

Nicholas Baugniet

Gillian Jones

David Walters

OXFORD

UNIVERSITY PRESS

OXFORD
UNIVERSITY PRESS

Great Clarendon Street, Oxford OX2 6DP

Oxford University Press is a department of the University of Oxford.
It furthers the University's objective of excellence in research, scholarship,
and education by publishing worldwide in
Oxford New York
Auckland Bangkok Buenos Aires
Cape Town Chennai Dar es Salaam Delhi Hong Kong Istanbul
Karachi Kolkata Kuala Lumpur Madrid Melbourne Mexico City Mumbai Nairobi
São Paulo Shanghai Taipei Tokyo Toronto

Oxford is a registered trade mark of Oxford University Press
in the UK and in certain other countries

ISBN 0 19 913410 3 School Edition
First published 2000
10 9 8 7 6 5
ISBN 0 19 913411 1 Bookshop Edition
First published 2000
15 14 13 12 11 10 9

A catalogue record for this book is available from the British Library.

The authors would like to thank Roger Hucthinson for his contribution
to the material on pages 52-57.

Editorial, design, and artwork by Hart McLeod, Cambridge

Illustrations by Tim Oliver and Kate Taylor

Printed in Great Britain

Acknowledgements

The publisher and authors would like to thank the following for permission
to reproduce photographs and other copyright material:

Front cover image by Tony Stone Images/Alan Thornton.

Every effort has been made to trace and contact copyright holders of
material reproduced in this book. Any omissions will be rectified in
subsequent printings if notice is given to the publisher.

Where to find the information you need

Contents

Joints and movement types

> *Joints are where bones meet. There are three types...*

Fixed or immovable joints

Technical name: synarthrosis

The bones at an immovable joint are not able to move. They interlock or overlap, and are held together by tough fibre.

> **Example:** the joints between plates (sutures) in the skull (cranium).

Freely movable joints

Technical name: diarthrosis

The bones at freely movable joints can move quite freely. These joints are also called synovial joints. A synovial, or freely movable, joint allows movement to occur, but may be restricted by the articular surfaces. There is a fluid-filled cavity which contains the ligaments and tendons that pass through the joint, as well as the cartilage. A synovial membrane encloses the synovial fluid which acts as a lubricant for the joint.

> **Examples:** shoulder, hip, knee, elbow.

Slightly movable joints

Technical name: amphiarthrosis

The bones at a slightly movable joint can only move a little. They are held together by straps called ligaments and joined by pads of gristly cartilage.

> **Example:** the joints between most vertebrae (backbone).

Cartilage

> protects bones and stops them knocking together.

> forms a cushion between bones at slightly movable joints (e.g. between vertebrae).

> forms a smooth, slippery coat on the ends of bones.

> acts as a shock absorber so the bones don't jar when you run and jump.

Ligaments

> are strong cords or straps that hold bones together.

> hold a joint in place.

> are slightly elastic – just enough to allow the bones to move the way they should.

Freely movable joints and their movements

There are six types...

1 Ball and sockets

The round end of one bone fits into a hollow in the other, and can turn in many directions.

> **Examples:**
> Shoulder (scapula-humerus): flexion, extension, abduction, adduction
> Hip (acetabulum-femur): rotation, circumduction

2 Hinge

The joint can swing open until it is straight, like a door hinge.

> **Examples:**
> Elbow: flexion and extension only (humerus-ulna)
> Fingers/toes: phalanges
> Shin bone/ankle: talus

3 Pivot

A ring on one bone fits over a peg on the other, allowing rotation.

> **Examples:**
> Neck joint between the atlas and axis: rotation only
> Elbow: rotation only (head of radius/head or ulna): supination/pronation

Movement types

Different joints allow different kinds of movement.
There are 12 kinds of movement in the human body.
Try doing them.

1 Flexion – bending

2 Extension – straightening

3 Plantar flexion – pointing the toes

4 Dorsi flexion – bringing the toes towards the tibia (leg)

5 Adduction – movement towards the body's midline

6 Abduction – movement from the body's midline

7 Circumduction – a combination of flexion, extension, adduction and abduction

8 Rotation – movement around the long axis of the bone (internal towards body axis; external away from body axis)

9 Pronation – turning the palm of the hand down

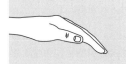

10 Supination – turning the palm up

11 Inversion – turning the sole of the foot inwards

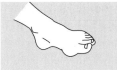

12 Eversion – turning the sole of the foot outwards

4 Condyloid

A bump on one bone sits in the hollow formed by another bone or bones. Movement is back and forward and from side to side. Ligaments prevent rotation.

Examples:
Wrist: flexion
Forearm bones – Carpals: extension
Femur and Tibia (structurally): adduction + adduction = circumduction
(Condyloid but acts like a hinge)

5 Saddle

Part of one bone is saddle shaped; the other bone glides on it. Movement is back and forward and from side to side.

Examples:
Thumb – apposition of thumb

6 Gliding

Flat surfaces can glide over each other, giving a limited movement in all directions.

Examples:
Carpals and metacarpals
Femur – Patella
Tarsals and metatarsals
Vertebrae – Ribs

Exam tips

You should be able to draw and label:
> knee joint
> hip joint
> ankle joint
> shoulder joint
> elbow joint
> spine
> wrist

The mechanics of movement

> *Newtonian principles that govern all movements.*

Levers

The joints of our skeleton not only allow movement, they also act as levers. The joint itself is used as the turning point, the fulcrum, to 'take the strain' of pulling one bone nearer, or away from, another bone.

The human body is a system of levers and pulleys that enable us to move. The levers rotate around a series of joints, with the force being provided by muscles attached to bones (acting as pulleys). The resistance comes in the form of body weight and any implement used for sport (e.g. a bat or racquet).

Levers have two functions:

1 To apply force (strength) to an object – the longer the lever distance from the force to fulcrum the greater the force generated.

2 To move the resistance a greater distance or through a greater range of movement. The closer the effort is to the fulcrum, the greater the distance moved.

Joints work most efficiently at around a 90° angle of pull. At low angles and at high angles (120°+) greater strength (effort) is required to maintain the efficiency of the action. Think of any sporting activity: which part of the swing requires the most effort?

Orders of levers

1st order lever

This is a lever where the fulcrum occurs between the effort and resistance.

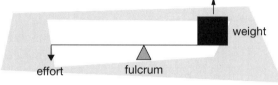

2nd order lever

This lever occurs where the load is between the effort and the fulcrum.

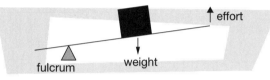

3rd order lever

This lever occurs where the effort lies between the fulcrum and resistance. This is very common in human movement.

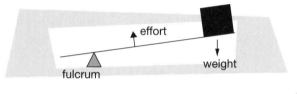

Motion

Force is used to move objects, to stop moving objects and to resist movement in stationary objects. Newton's Laws of Motion rely on an understanding of force.

> Force can be applied with varying sizes and is measured in Newtons (N). This depends on the mass of the body and the effect of gravity.
> Force can be applied in varying directions – the direction of the force dictates the direction of motion of an object if applied to its centre of gravity. This is also known as **linear motion**.
> When force is applied off-centre, it produces movement that is known as **angular motion**.

Newton's 1st Law

'A body will continue in its state of rest or motion unless another force acts on it.'

All objects have an inertia which must be overcome to change its state of motion (alter its velocity). For example, the 'jack' in bowls will only come to rest when friction force from the grass or mat has overcome its inertia of movement.

Newton's 2nd Law

'The rate of change of velocity (acceleration) of an object is directly proportional to the force acting on it.'

In sport we can propel objects further by imparting greater momentum to that object.

momentum = mass x velocity

For example, a golf ball will travel further if you hit it with the same force but with a heavier club.

Newton's 3rd Law

'Every action has an equal and opposite reaction.'

When one object produces force against another object, it exerts an equal force back in the opposite direction. For example, when a sprinter pushes against the blocks at the start of a race, they push back with equal force, propelling the runner forward.

Centre of gravity, rotation and balance

> *Maintaining balance and initiating rotation.*

Centre of gravity

This is the point in any object where all of its mass (weight) is said to be concentrated.

In an object – known as 'a uniform body' – the **centre of gravity** will be at its geometric centre.

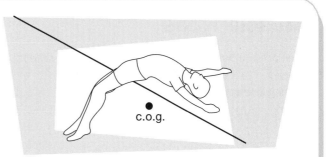

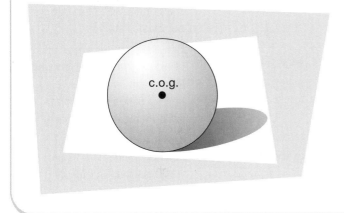

In the human body, the centre of gravity is constantly changing with movement. This is because the centre of gravity is determined by the distribution of mass and the density of the body.

The centre of gravity remains inside the physical body most of the time. However, in some activities the performer deliberately moves the centre of gravity outside the body to improve technique: for example, the high jumper arching over the bar.

Rotation

Rotation, or the turning of a body, occurs when force is applied to that body though not through the centre of

gravity. When this force occurs, angular motion and rotation can occur around the centre of gravity.

A forward roll is initiated when the centre of gravity moves outside the area of support by a force that does not act through the centre of gravity. The force from the leg muscles pushing onto the ground and the ground returning that force to the feet enables you to shift your centre of gravity. This rotation continues into the forward roll.

Balance

A state of balance is achieved when the centre of gravity is over the area of support for the body. It allows you to hold a position without wobbling or falling over.

The stability of the balance is affected by the height of the centre of gravity. Lowering the height of the centre of gravity makes a balance much more stable. Headstands are easier to maintain with bent legs initially, than with legs stretched straight. Crouching low makes you harder to knock over in contact sports.

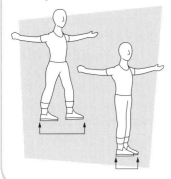

The larger the area of support the easier it is to maintain balance. Standing upright, legs astride is more balanced than on legs close together, or on one leg.

Muscles and muscle function (1)

> *The means of converting chemical energy into mechanical energy.*

Muscle types

Every movement that takes place in your body depends on muscles. They contract and lengthen to produce movement. Muscles convert chemical energy into mechanical energy.

There are three types of muscle:

1 Cardiac

> Called **myocardium** (or cardiac striped) **muscle**.

> Found only in the heart, where linked fibres act in unison.

> Acts as a single sheet of muscle because between the single cells is a very thin disc which has very low resistance to neural impulse (intercalated discs).

> Involuntary and has its own blood supply.

> The heart generates its own impulse to beat, so is called **myogenic**.

> Obeys the 'all-or-nothing law'.

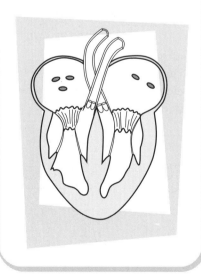

2 Visceral

> Involuntary muscles, because they work without you thinking about it. Controlled by involuntary parts of the nervous system.

> Associated with viscera (internal organs such as arteries, stomach, bowel).

> Composed of minute, spindle-shaped cells whose fibres are so fine they appear smooth.

> Often form circular or longitudinal coats.

> Each muscle fibre does *not* have a separate nerve to control it but the entire sheet is served by a nerve **plexus**.

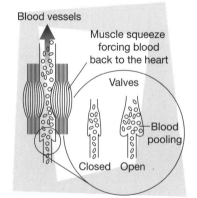

Blood vessels

Muscle squeeze forcing blood back to the heart

Valves

Blood pooling

Closed   Open

When the visceral muscle in the artery walls contracts, blood is squirted along the artery.

When the visceral muscle in the stomach wall contracts, it pushes food along.

3 Skeletal

> Attached to the skeleton, directly or indirectly.

> Controlled by voluntary parts of the nervous system.

> Composed of large, grooved cells bound together into bundles or sheets.

> Skeletal muscles are attached at their **origins** and **insertions** by a white, fibrous tissue which forms **tendons** or **aponeuroses**.

> The fascia is a tough, fibrous, connective tissue which surrounds muscle bundles.

> During movement the origins remain fixed whilst the insertions move.

> Each muscle fibre is served by a nerve fibre that is attached to the muscle via a 'motor end plate'. Skeletal muscles obey the 'all-or-nothing law'.

> The contraction of the whole muscle is proportional to the number of fibres stimulated.

> Muscle tone is maintained by a small number of fibres being stimulated constantly.

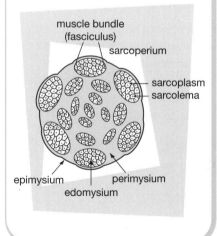

muscle bundle (fasciculus)

sarcoperium

sarcoplasm
sarcolema

epimysium

perimysium

edomysium

Muscle arrangements

Muscles are normally arranged in pairs so that when one is contracting the other is relaxing. As an example, when the biceps contracts, the triceps muscle relaxes – and the lower arm is raised. Then when the triceps contracts, the biceps must relax or the lower arm will not be lowered.

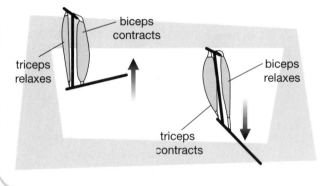

> Muscles that cause the joints to bend are known as **flexors**.

> Muscles that cause the joints to straighten are called **extensors**.

> The muscle that shortens to move the joint is the **prime mover** or **agonist**, whilst the muscle that relaxes is called the **antagonist**.

> Muscles which act as agonist for one movement, act as antagonist muscle for the opposite movement.

> Additionally, muscles which stabilise the origin, so only the insertion moves, are called **fixators** and **synergists**. Fixator muscles hold joints in position so the origin and insertion are on opposite sides of a stabilised joint. Synergist muscles hold the body in position to enable agonists to work.

Muscular contraction

There are four forms of muscle contraction:

1 Isometric (equal length) or static muscle contraction

There is generally no movement resulting from this contraction.

> **Examples:** pushing against a fixed object (e.g. a wall); pushing one hand against the other; arm wrestling.

> Force of muscle contraction = force expressed by resistance

2 Isotonic – concentric muscle contraction

Equal control. The muscles contract at a speed controlled by the individual. This produces positive movement (shortening of length), which closely mimics the sporting situation to which the training is applied.

3 Isokinetic – concentric muscle contraction

Equal speed. The point at which the force acts or moves at a constant speed. Specialist machines are required.

4 Polymetrics – eccentric muscle contractions

It has been found that if maximum effort is put into an exercise whilst a muscle is lengthening, then the muscle exerts a much bigger force. This is eccentric or negative exercise.

> **Examples:** bounding exercises; running downhill.

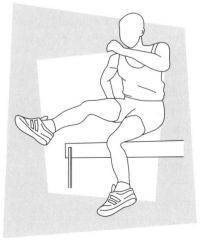

Muscles and muscle function (2)

> *What separates sprinters from marathon runners?*

Types of muscle fibre

By themselves muscle fibres are not very strong, but when lots of them are wrapped together in bundles they make a powerful mass of muscles.

There are two main types of muscle fibre.

Type 1: Slow twitch fibres

> Slow twitch fibres contract at a rate of about 20% slower than fast twitch fibres.

> They are smaller than fast twitch fibres and have smaller motor neurones, thus they generate force comparatively slowly.

> Slow twitch fibres do not fatigue as easily as fast twitch fibres, which makes them perfect for most low-level activities.

Type 2: Fast twitch fibres

Can be further sub-divided:

1 Type 2a: Fast Twitch High Oxidative Glycolytic (FOG) – used for longer sprint events.

2 Type 2b: Fast Twitch Glycolytic (FTG) – used for short sprint events.

Type 2a (FOG) have a greater resistance to fatigue than Type 2b (FTG). This is entirely due to endurance training which encourages muscular adaptation.

> All muscles have a mixture of fast and slow twitch fibres.

Fibre-type characteristics

Characteristic	Type 1: slow twitch	Type 2: fast twitch	
Size		*FOG (2a) small*	*FTG (2b) large*
Myoglobin Content	High	High	Low
Capillary Density	High	Midway/High	Low
Mitochondrial Density	High	Midway	Low
Activity during low intensity exercise	High	Midway	Low
Glycogen Stores	Low	High	High
Phosphocreatine Content	Low	Midway	High
Fatigue Level	Low	Midway	High
Contractile Time	Slow	Midway	High
Relaxation Time	Slow	Midway	High
Activity during high intensity exercise	Slow	High	High

An individual muscle is composed of hundreds of **muscle fibres**.

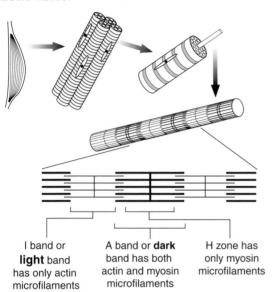

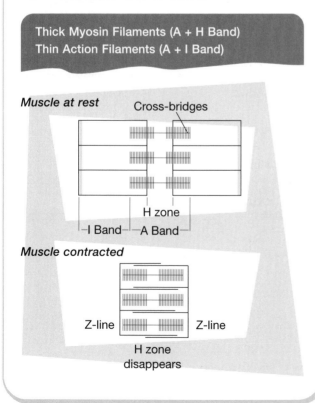

I band or **light** band has only actin microfilaments	A band or **dark** band has both actin and myosin microfilaments	H zone has only myosin microfilaments

Each muscle fibre is composed of many myofibrils.

A myofibril has a distinctive banding pattern due to **microfilaments**.

Sarcomere is the functional basic unit of a myofibril. Thousands of sarcomeres form a long chain in each myofibril.

The Z membrane indicates the boundaries between sarcomeres. The longitudinal protein filaments cause the striated appearance of muscle.

Thick Myosin Filaments (A + H Band)
Thin Action Filaments (A + I Band)

Muscle at rest

Cross-bridges

H zone
I Band   A Band

Muscle contracted

Z-line   Z-line

H zone
disappears

Huxley's sliding filament theory

In the sarcomere the alternating bands of light and dark areas are caused because of the different thicknesses of actin and myosin. They give clues as to how Huxley's theory works:

> Areas of thicker myosin (A Band, H Zone) form the middle of the sarcomere.

> Areas of thinner actin (also troponin and tropomyosin) (I Band) form the outer parts of the sarcomere and attach to Z discs.

When an impulse arrives at the muscle cell, this triggers the release of calcium ions from 'T' vesicles (sacs within the cytoplasm of cells). The calcium ions bind to troponin and cause the binding sites on actin to be exposed.

Adenosine triphosphate (ATP) – main supplier of metabolic energy in living cells – is broken down and energy is released. This energy is used to power the myosin heads attachment to actin sites.

These cross-bridges (actin-myosin) attach, detach and re-attach further along the actin filament – pulling the actin past the myosin. This has the effect of shortening the length of the sarcomere, as the Z discs are pulled closer together – shortening the muscle.

Muscle contraction requires Ca^{2+} ions and ATP

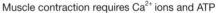

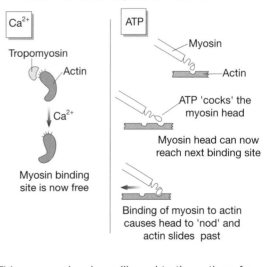

Ca^{2+}

Tropomyosin
Actin

Ca^{2+}

Myosin binding site is now free

ATP

Myosin
Actin

ATP 'cocks' the myosin head

Myosin head can now reach next binding site

Binding of myosin to actin causes head to 'nod' and actin slides past

This process has been likened to the action of a person climbing a rope. The arms and legs represent the cross bridges. Movement occurs because the limbs reach and grasp then pull, break contact then reach and grasp then pull and so on; the cross bridges do the same.

Controlling muscular action

> *How the body applies just enough strength to do a job.*

A motor unit producing movement

A neurone (or neuron) forms the basic cellular unit of the nervous system. It is capable of carrying nerve impulses to muscles. A motor neurone controls large numbers of individual fibres – together they form a **motor unit**.

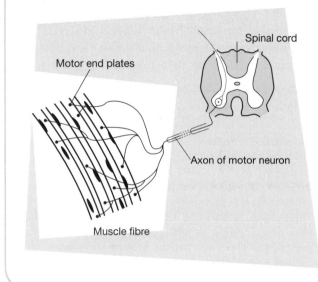

The axon branches as it reaches the muscle. The branches connect with a structure called the **motor end plate**.

Messages sent along motor neurones are electrochemical in nature. The generation of the messages relies upon an 'action potential' occurring in the axon. This occurs where the axon becomes 'leaky' and K^+ (potassium) ions diffuse out and N^+ (nitrogen) ions diffuse in.

To increase the speed of transfer, 'saltatory conduction' is used. This involves ion exchange occurring only at nodes on the axon known as 'nodes of Ranvier'[1].

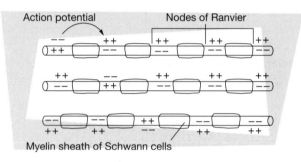

[1]named after Louis-Antoine Ranvier (1835-1922); the Schwann cells are named after Theodor Schwann (1810-1882)

The function of motor end plates

Motor end plates transfer the electrical impulse from motor neurones to muscle fibres.

> There is a delay of approximately 0.5 ms (microseconds) in order for the release of Acetylcholine (the carrier of the signal) from the synaptic knob.

> An area of depolarisation travels down the muscle cell which initiates the release of Ca^{2+} (calcium ions) from the 'T' vesicles (see page 9).

> This, in turn, causes the sliding filaments to begin their action.

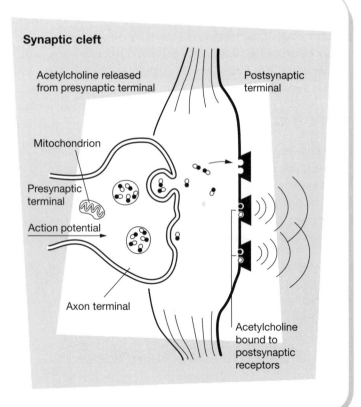

Motor neurone firing patterns

Neurones are of different types depending on their position in the nervous system. Motor neurones have short dendrons and long axons. Nerve impulses that are carried along the neurone are fired in various patterns.

Here are some of those firing patterns.

Muscle twitch

Stimuli received by neurone pools are transmitted to different motor units, which may not act in unison. The stimulus must be sufficiently strong to activate one motor unit in order to produce any contraction. **ALL** of the muscle fibres in that motor unit will contract maximally for a fraction of a second ('all-or-nothing law').

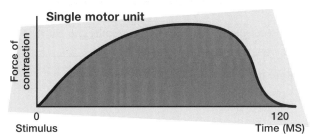

Graduation of contraction

Muscles contract for longer than a fraction of a second when a stimulus occurs that activates many motor neurones (different motor units will be involved, not necessarily in succession). This allows muscles to exert forces of graded strength. This skill is learned over time and through varied practice.

Wave summation

The strength of a muscle contraction can be increased in another way. If a second impulse is received by a neurone pool very quickly, there will not be time for relaxation before the next contraction starts. This increase in rate of stimulation to produce stronger contractions is **wave summation**.

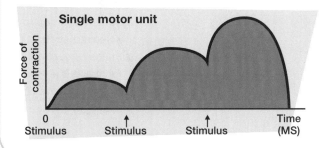

Absolute contraction

If stimuli arrive so fast there is no time for any relaxation, a state of 'absolute contraction' occurs.

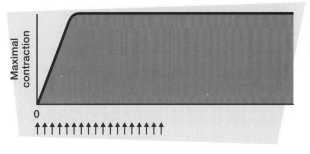

Spatial summation

This is the term given to the phenomenon of different motor units being stimulated across the whole muscle to produce contraction. Spatial summation allows the use of stores of ATP (adenosine triphosphate) to be shared around the whole muscle, thus reducing fatigue.

The *staggered* nature of the working of the motor units is an important factor in maintaining sustained contraction. Some motor units will be relaxing (and recovering) whilst others are contracting, which allows long periods of contraction.

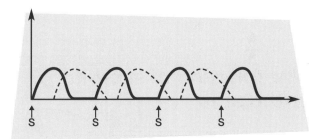

(Note: all muscle action requires the development of isometric tension in order to overcome inertia and to initiate movement.)

Co-ordinated contraction relies on the factors above and sensory feedback which adjusts contraction. These are produced by specialist proprioceptors and nerves, e.g.

Golgi Tendon Apparatus + Muscle Spindles

The information received plays a role in decision making.

Reciprocal innervation is the constant adjustment of tension in antagonistic muscle groups based on sensory information from each muscle group. The **cerebellum** (brain) acts as a 'sorting office' for information which is then relayed to muscles to produce fine movement control.

The heart – structure

The body's pump

The heart is a muscular pump that beats nearly 4 million times a year. It pumps blood around the miles of arteries, veins and capillaries that make up the circulatory system.

The aorta carries oxygenated blood from the left ventricle to the systemic circulation. It is a typical elastic (conducting) artery with a wall that is relatively thick, and with more elastic fibres than smooth muscle. This allows the aorta to accommodate the surges of blood associated with the alternative contraction and relaxation of the heart.

The **pressure** generated by the left ventricle is greater than that generated by the right ventricle as the systemic circuit is more extensive than the pulmonary circuit.

The pressure generated by the atria is less than that generated by the ventricles since the distance from atria to ventricles is less than that from ventricles to circulatory system.

The same **volume** of blood passes through each side of the heart, so circulating volumes are also equal in the pulmonary and systemic circuits.

> When resting, the heart beats around 70 times a minute.

> It beats 100,000 times in a day.

> 7500 litres of blood pass through the heart each day – enough to fill a small road tanker.

Structures

Pericardium – the closed sac that surrounds the heart. It is fluid filled to reduce the effects of friction and to protect the heart.

Myocardium – cardiac muscle – composed of muscle cells with a single nucleus, but many mitochondria.

Endocardium – smooth tissues inside the heart chambers to aid blood flow.

Epicardium – outer layer of tissue of the heart. Links with inner layer of pericardium.

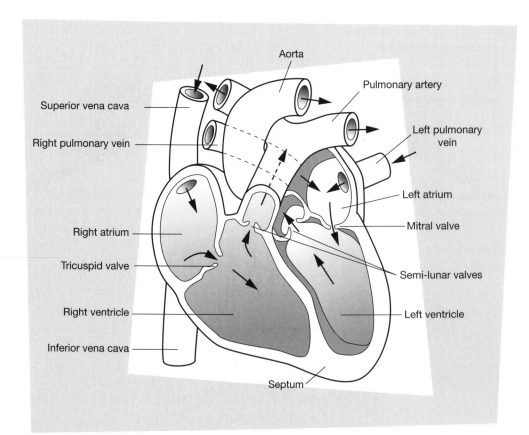

- Aorta
- Pulmonary artery
- Superior vena cava
- Left pulmonary vein
- Right pulmonary vein
- Left atrium
- Mitral valve
- Right atrium
- Tricuspid valve
- Semi-lunar valves
- Right ventricle
- Left ventricle
- Inferior vena cava
- Septum

Starling's Law of the heart

Cardiac output is dependent on venous return (i.e. the amount of blood returned to the right side of the heart). During exercise venous return increases, thus cardiac output increases. This is because the myocardium is stretched and then contracts with greater force due to the increased stretch. The stimulus to contract more forcibly is the greater stretching of the fibres.

Heartbeat

Blood is supplied to the heart muscle itself via coronary arteries that branch from the aorta. Deoxygenated blood from the heart muscles is fed directly back to the right atrium via coronary veins and coronary sinus.

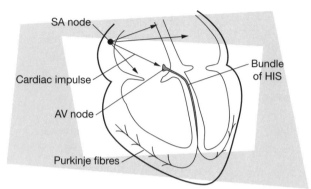

The heartbeat is initiated by electrical impulses which originate from the heart's 'pacemaker', the **sino-atrial node** (particularly excitable tissue in the wall of the right atrium; labelled as SA node). The impulse travels down the myocardium of the atrium until it reaches the **atrio-ventricular node** (AV node). A short delay occurs to allow atrial systole – see page 14 – to complete. The impulse then enters specialist tissues called **'Bundles of HIS'** which branch through the septum as **Purkinje fibres**[1]. These connect to myocardium fibres which cause the ventricles to contract (ventricular systole).

This process can be seen by tracing the electrical signals in the heart using an ECG (electrocardiogram).

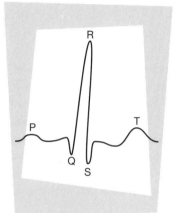

P = a wave of electrical energy just before the atria contract – impulse travelling from SA node to AV node.

Q, R, S = a wave of electrical energy just before the ventricles contract – impulse travelling from AV node along bundles of HIS and Purkinje fibres.

T = repolarisation of ventricle walls before relaxation (diastole).

1 **Intrinsic heart** rate is about 78 beats per minute.

2 **External (extrinsic)** factors may modify the basic heart rate:
> **vagus nerve** decreases heart rate
> **accelerator nerve** increases heart rate
> **adrenaline** and **thyroxine** increase heart rate.

1   Named after Jan Evangelista Purkinje (1787-1869)

Stroke volume (SV) – the amount of blood ejected from the heart when the ventricles contract[1].
(All figures approximate)

Untrained at rest	70 ml	Untrained maximal exercise	113 ml
Trained at rest	100 ml	Trained maximal exercise	179 ml

Heart rate (HR) – number of ventricular contractions in one minute

Untrained at rest	70 beats/minute	Untrained maximal exercise	195 beats/minute
Trained at rest	50 beats/minute	Trained maximal exercise	195 beats/minute

Cardiac output (Q) – the amount of blood ejected from the heart in one minute

Untrained at rest	5,000 ml (5 litres)	Untrained maximal exercise	22,000 ml (22 litres)
Trained at rest	5,000 ml (5 litres)	Trained maximal exercise	35,000 ml (35 litres)

Q = SV x HR

1   Stroke volume is increased due to (training) exercise as both the size of the heart and the muscle wall thickness increase. The larger and more powerful the heart, the fewer times it needs to beat in order to circulate the same amount of blood. Reduced heart rate at rest is known as 'bradycardia'.

The heart – cardiac cycle

> *How the heart works.*

Cardiac cycle

Two phases in the cycle:
> Relaxation – diastole 0.5 secs
> Contraction – systole 0.3 secs

The cycle starts

Systole

The SA node initiates an impulse causing a wave of contraction across the atrial myocardium, forcing the remaining blood out of the atria into the ventricles. Semi-lunar valves remain closed, but atrio-ventricular valves close after the passage of blood. This causes one of the heart sounds. The 'lub' of 'lub dub'. The impulse then reaches the AV node which then spreads a second contraction through the ventricle walls. Rising ventricular pressure forces open the semi-lunar valves to the lungs and systemic arteries.

Once the blood has left the heart and the contraction ceases the semi-lunar valves snap shut causing the 'dub' sound in the heart.

Diastole

Right and left atria fill with blood and the atrioventricular valves are closed (mitral & tricuspid).

Rising atrial pressure forces open the atrioventricular valves and the ventricles begin to fill. The semi-lunar valves to the aorta and pulmonary arteries are closed.

Heart rate regulation

This occurs via the sympathetic and parasympathetic nervous systems. These originate in the cardiac centre of the medulla oblongata (brain stem) – they work antagonistically. The effect of exercise is to speed up the heart rate (HR). This is achieved by the sympathetic nerves transmitting impulses to the SA node and the release of **norepinephrine**, a transmitter substance.

Baroreceptors located in the carotid artery and aorta respond to increased blood pressure by sending messages back to the cardiac centre. This, in turn, sends out impulses via the vagus nerve (parasympathetic nerves) to the SA node to slow down the heart rate.

THIS IS NEGATIVE FEEDBACK CONTROL.

Other factors affecting heart rate include:
> raised temperature
> hormonal release (e.g. adrenaline – this substance redirects blood flow and increases glycolysis)
> excess potassium can slow down HR
> age – HR drops with age one beat per year
> gender – females tend to have higher heart rates than males.

Heart rate is dependent upon a balance between sympathetic nerves (SNS) and parasympathetic nerves (PNS), which adjust to changing conditions.

Information received from peripheral sensors – e.g. baroreceptors (blood pressure); chemoreceptors (chemical sensors) and proprioceptors (in joints and tissues) – in the cardiac centre of the medulla oblongata is interpreted and redirected via SNS and PNS to the SA node.

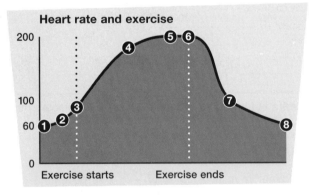

Heart rate and exercise

Exercise starts   Exercise ends

1   Resting heart rate 60–70 beats/minute.
2   Pre-exercise anticipatory rise (adrenaline release).
3   Exercise begins – blood pressure increases, CO_2 content increases.
4   Steep rise in heart rate as exercise increases in intensity.
5   A plateau occurs near to age-predicted maximum heart rate despite an increase in exercise intensity.
6   Exercise ends and the heart rate immediately begins to rapidly fall, blood pressure decreases, CO_2 content decreases, venous return reduces.
7   Longer recovery period close to resting levels to help clear the by-products of tissue respiration.
8   Return to normal.

The body's transport system – blood

> *The fluid of life.*

Blood is the body's internal transport system. The blood vessels carry the raw materials along the network of arteries, veins and capillaries to all the consumers of the body – from major organs to each and every individual living cell.

What is blood?

If blood is spun for a few minutes in a high-speed centrifuge it separates into two layers:

1 Plasma (55%)

Straw-coloured fluid. At least 90% water, dissolved in which are salts, glucose, fatty acids, waste products, enzymes and hormones.

2 Cells (corpuscles) (45%)

Eosinophils   Neutrophils   Basophils   Lymphocytes

Red cells   Platelets (Thrombocytes)   Monocytes

> **red cells**, or **erythrocytes** – most numerous; red colour due to presence of haemoglobin (oxygen-carrying protein); relatively short lived. Carry oxygen (O_2), carbon dioxide (CO_2) and carbon monoxide (CO) around the body. Typical lifespan of a red cell is 19–20 days.

> **white cells**, or **leucocytes** – help to fight disease and injury in the body. There are various types: neutrophils (most abundant; very short lived; migrate from blood to tissues; replaced at the rate of 100000 million every day); monocytes (largest type; spend a short time in circulatory system before moving into the tissues); lymphocytes (30%; produced in bone marrow but continue to develop in lymph nodes, thymus gland and spleen; produce antibodies).

> **platelets**, or **thrombocytes** – fragments of cells which are involved in blood clotting.

> **basophils** – secrete large amounts of histamine (which increases swelling) and heparin (which helps to keep a balance between blood clotting and not clotting).

> **eosinophils** – help control the allergic response (e.g. secrete enzymes which activate histamine); numbers increase during an allergic reaction and in response to some parasitic infections.

Function: transport

> Food from alimentary canal
> Oxygen from lungs to tissues
> Waste from tissues to the excretory surface
> Hormones from the endocrine system
> White corpuscles to fight infection
> Heat.

Function: protection

> Salts to provide a buffering action to protect cells
> White corpuscles to fight disease
> Clotting properties
> White corpuscles to help wounds heal.

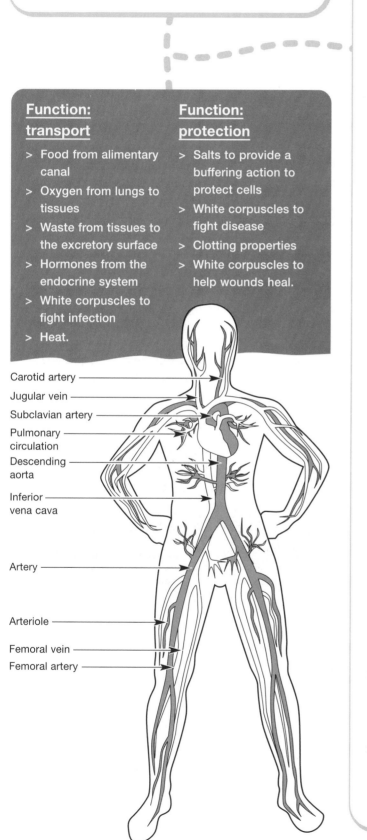

Carotid artery
Jugular vein
Subclavian artery
Pulmonary circulation
Descending aorta
Inferior vena cava
Artery
Arteriole
Femoral vein
Femoral artery

The body's transport system – blood vessels

> *The motorways of the body.*

2 Arterioles

These have the same structure as arteries but are much narrower.

Function: to control blood flow into capillaries (due to vasomotor control).

1 Arteries

An artery is surrounded by 'smooth' muscle which controls the size of the lumen through which the blood flows. It carries oxygenated blood under pressure. This flows in spurts as the heart beats.

Thick elastic walls have three layers:

> **interna** – forms the inner lining of the vessel with endothelium

> **media** – formed of smooth muscle and elastin

> **externa** – formed of collagen and elastin to allow the walls to be elastic and cope with changes in blood volume.

3 Capillaries

Smallest blood vessels in the body – they pass through most muscle and other tissues.

Capillary bed – total capillary structure within a muscle or organ. The number of capillaries can be increased by training, thus O_2 and other nutrients can be delivered efficiently. Total cross-section of capillary bed is much greater than a single artery, so the speed of blood flow is dramatically reduced.

This allows greater efficiency in diffusion of O_2 into muscle tissue and diffusion of CO_2 out across the single cell layer of endothelium tissue. Once CO_2 and other waste products have been collected, the blood leaves the capillary bed and enters venules.

6 Vena cava

The final veins before blood gets back to the heart.

5 Veins

Blood vessels carrying deoxygenated blood from capillaries back to the heart. They have a muscular coat, which affects the tone of the veins due to venomotor control. This allows changes in capacity of blood flow.

4 Venules

These begin the journey of deoxygenated blood back to the heart. The blood pressure is low, so the blood has a smooth flow. This is achieved because of:

> smooth flow from the capillaries

> pressure from surrounding organs (e.g. working muscles – important for cool down)

> valves to prevent backflow

> suction caused by decreasing pressure in thorax due to inhalation.

Blood flow in muscles

The rate of blood flow around the body depends on a number of variables:

> physical activity – muscles demand more O_2
> cardiac output
> circulation.

Blood pressure also changes due to:

> cardiac output
> peripheral resistance – altered by vasodilation and vasoconstriction[1], by blood viscosity (thickness), and by the changing shape and size of arterioles. Precapillary sphincters (circular tract of muscles) also control blood flow to capillaries. Messages come from the vasomotor and venomotor centres – both centres are located in the medulla oblongata and are regulated by sympathetic and parasympathetic nervous systems.

Vasomotor control

A fall in blood pressure reduces stimulation of baroreceptors. The vasomotor centre sends nerve impulses to arterioles causing them to vasoconstrict; hence an increase in blood pressure and heart rate.

An increase in blood pressure increases stimulation of baroreceptors, which causes the vasomotor centre to send out more impulses to cause vasodilation, so reducing blood pressure.

Venomotor control

Veins can alter their shape on receipt of signals from the sympathetic and parasympathetic nervous systems by altering the venomotor tone of their muscular 'coats'.

Venous return

The volume of blood leaving the heart has a direct relationship with the pumping action of the heart. Blood flow in the veins also increases. (Thus venous return.) Veins contain approximately ⅗th of circulating blood at any one time. Venous return must be in excess of the rest of the blood in the body in order to maintain steady blood flow. During exercise, the working muscles squeeze the veins, thus increasing venal return (muscle pump). During inspiration (breathing in), the reduction in pressure in the thorax aids venous return as the blood will move to low pressure areas (respiratory pump).

Stroke volume levels out before maximum effort is achieved.

Tissue fluid during exercise

High blood pressure at the arteriole end of the capillary bed forces fluid through the capillary wall into the cell spaces. Tissue cells extract O_2 + glucose; they excrete CO_2, etc. where blood pressure is lowest at the venous end of the capillary bed.

> Exercise increases systolic blood pressure
> ▼
> thus increasing tissue fluid production
> ▼
> thus more nutrients are available for tissue respiration.

---

1 Ability of blood vessels, particularly capillaries, to increase (vasodilation) or decrease (vasoconstriction) in diameter under nervous or hormonal control. When you are at risk of overheating, vasodilation of capillaries in the skin allows more blood to flow to the surface of the body, where heat can be lost by radiation. When cold, vasoconstriction prevents blood from flowing near the body surface, and heat is conserved deeper in the body.

Blood flow

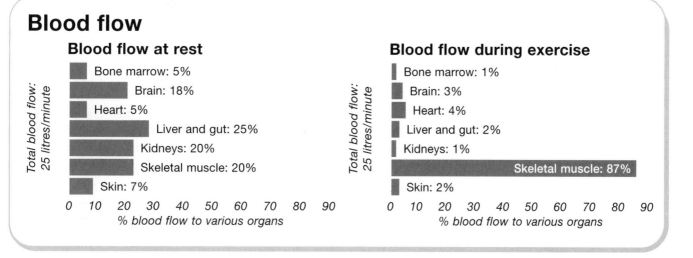

Blood flow at rest

Total blood flow: 25 litres/minute

- Bone marrow: 5%
- Brain: 18%
- Heart: 5%
- Liver and gut: 25%
- Kidneys: 20%
- Skeletal muscle: 20%
- Skin: 7%

0 10 20 30 40 50 60 70 80 90
% blood flow to various organs

Blood flow during exercise

Total blood flow: 25 litres/minute

- Bone marrow: 1%
- Brain: 3%
- Heart: 4%
- Liver and gut: 2%
- Kidneys: 1%
- Skeletal muscle: 87%
- Skin: 2%

0 10 20 30 40 50 60 70 80 90
% blood flow to various organs

The mechanics of breathing

> *How the body causes movement of air in and out of the lungs.*

Inspiration and expiration

Inspiration and expiration are caused by the changes in air pressure inside the lungs (i.e. intra-pulmonary). This is relative to atmospheric pressure. The changes in pressure are caused by muscular action of the intercostal muscles and diaphragm. (This has implications for high- and low-pressure training and physical activity.)

Inspiration occurs as a result of changes in the size of the thorax, due to muscular action that reduces pressure inside the pleural membranes. This reduction is enough to cause air to rush into the low-pressure area of the lungs. Expiration is caused by an increase of pressure on the pleural membrane from the falling ribs and returning diaphragm. Also the alveoli, which have been stretched during inspiration, recoil – forcing air out of the lungs.

The respiratory muscles

1 Primary

> 11 pairs of intercostal muscles between the 12 pairs of ribs, arranged in two layers (internal and external).
> Internal muscle fibres attach from the lower margin of the rib above the upper margin of the rib below. The upper attachment is nearer the sternum.
> External fibres lie on top of internal fibres and point in the opposite direction.

As the first rib is fixed when the external fibres contract, the ribs can move towards the fixed rib (i.e. an upward and outward movement), thus causing the thoracic cage to expand. During quiet breathing, gravity returns the cage to its normal position, thus causing *expiration*. (Intercostal nerves originate in the medulla oblongata.)

Diaphragm: sheet of muscle that forms the floor of the thoracic cavity. It attaches to the vertebrae column, ribs and sternum, and radiates from a central tendon. The diaphragm is innervated by phrenic nerves. When contracting, the central tendon is pulled down, thus enlarging the thoracic cavity (reducing pressure) – causing *inhalation*.

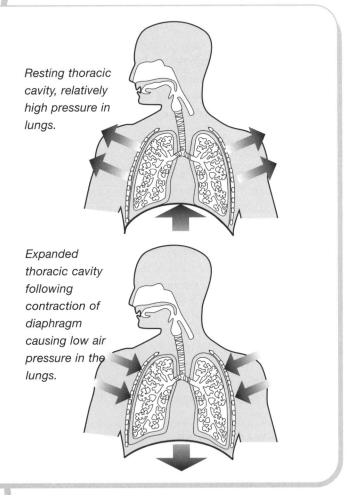

Resting thoracic cavity, relatively high pressure in lungs.

Expanded thoracic cavity following contraction of diaphragm causing low air pressure in the lungs.

2 Secondary (during exercise only)

At rest, when air requirements are low, there is no need for violent breathing movements. Heavier demands (e.g. during exercise) require contraction of the external intercostal muscles (see right).

Abdominal muscles force air out of the lungs during expiration and the internal intercostal muscles aid gravity by contracting, reducing the thorax dimensions.

Scaleni + Sternocleidomastoids contract
▼
raising first rib and sternum.

Trapezius + Back and Neck Extensors also contract
▼
increase in size of thorax.

Chemical and nervous regulation of the breathing mechanism

Breathing rates are controlled subconsciously by the medulla oblongata. The **apneustic centre** controls inspiration and the **pneumotaxic centre** controls expiration. Inspiration occurs due to an increased rate of firing of the inspiratory neurones and the recruitment of new motor units. Expiration is initiated by the abrupt cessation of the neurones firing.

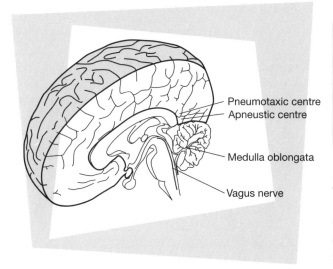

Pneumotaxic centre
Apneustic centre
Medulla oblongata
Vagus nerve

Excess inspiration is limited by the activation of stretch receptors in the bronchioles and bronchi which, when stimulated, send impulses via the vagus nerve to the medulla oblongata. These impulses either cause inspiration to be inhibited and or expiration to be stimulated. This is known as the **Hering–Breuer Reflex**.

1   Hg = chemical symbol for mercury; air pressure is measured on instruments using mercury (e.g. barometer).

Chemical controls

Peripheral chemoreceptors in the carotid arteries and the aorta respond to chemical changes in the blood – by sending impulses to the respiratory centres in the medulla oblongata.

Oxygen (O_2)

If partial pressure of O_2 falls below a certain level (60 mm Hg[1]), there is a marked increase in ventilation. This is because at 60 mm Hg **haemoglobin** is 90% saturated and transportation is still efficient, below this threshold oxygen transport is severely affected.

> **Haemoglobin:** protein composed of 4 chains, each of which contains a single atom of iron. It is with the iron atom that a molecule of O_2 combines; so each haemoglobin molecule can combine with 4 molecules of O_2. When all the iron atoms in a group of haemoglobin molecules are combined with O_2, the haemoglobin is said to be saturated (100%).

Carbon dioxide (CO_2)

Increases in CO_2 in the arteries results in an increase of carbonic acid in blood. Bicarbonate[2] buffering occurs and hydrogen (H^+) ions are formed. Increased hydrogen ion concentration stimulates increased ventilation; decreased concentrations inhibit ventilation.

Hydrogen ion concentration

When this occurs for reasons other than increased CO_2 level in blood (e.g. accumulation of lactic acid during exercise), this induces **hyperventilation**. The rate of excretion of CO_2 is increased, thus lower arterial levels of CO_2 and hydrogen ions.

2   Bicarbonate is the traditional name for hydrogencarbonate (acid salt of carbonic acid in which only one of the hydrogen atoms has been replaced).

How much air do you breathe?

> Tidal volume (TV): volume of air you breathe in (or out) with each breath.

> Respiratory rate (RR): number of breaths you take per minute.

> Minute volume (MV): volume of air you breathe in per minute.

> All three increase during exercise.

MV = TV x RR

For a typical 18-year-old		
	At rest	*During exercise*
TV (litres)	0.5	2.5
RR (breaths/min.)	12	30
MV (litres/min.)	6	75

Gas exchange in lungs

> *Getting oxygen from the atmosphere to the body's tissues.*

How air changes in your lungs

Air in

> about 21% oxygen

> about 79% nitrogen

> a tiny amount of carbon dioxide

> a little water vapour

Air out

> about 17% oxygen

> about 79% nitrogen

> 3% carbon dioxide

> a lot of water vapour

The respiration system works in conjunction with the vascular (blood transport) system in the process of gas exchange. Oxygen is transported from the lung alveoli to the working tissue cells (ultimate destination the mitochondria), whilst CO_2 travels in the opposite direction within the blood.

During inspiration, atmospheric air rushes into the lungs to equalise the pressures. It fills the alveoli sacs. Surrounding some of these sacs is a dense network of capillaries rich in blood. The air enters these sacs at rest. During exercise, there is a greater amount of air inspired; some must go to alveoli poorly supplied with blood, therefore O_2 is under-utilised. However, exercise induces an increase in the density of the capillaries within the lungs (and muscles) which effectively increases the surface area for O_2 exchange – thus more O_2 is utilised.

Gas moves in and out of the circulatory system by the process of **diffusion** (molecules move from areas of high concentration [pressure] to areas of low concentration [pressure] across the thin membrane separating alveoli and capillaries). In the capillaries about 98.5% of the O_2 combines with haemoglobin (Hb) for transportation. Diffusion is aided because the red corpuscles of blood are squeezed flatter in the tiny capillaries, thus increasing their surface area.

Partial pressure oxygen (pO_2)

Atmospheric air is a mixture of gases. At sea level the total pressure of the molecules of these gases is 760 mm Hg. Approximately 21% of air is oxygen, thus the amount of pressure applied by O_2 is 760 x 0.21 = 159.9 mm Hg (160 mm Hg). This is called the partial pressure of oxygen (pO_2). Because the molecules in air are so far apart they do not influence each other.

Partial pressure oxygen (pO_2)

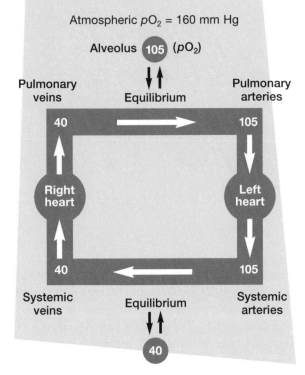

At each inspiration about 350 ml of air enters the lungs, to be added to the 2500 ml already contained there. The oxygen concentration is therefore diluted, thus alveoli O_2 has a partial pressure of about 105 mm Hg. Alveoli partial pressure remains fairly constant as inspiration raises pO_2 but decreases CO_2 – the amounts of change are insignificant as the amounts of air are relatively small compared with the air already held in the lungs.

The most important factor controlling the O_2 saturation of Hb is the partial pressure of O_2 in blood plasma (the concentration of dissolved O_2).

> As plasma oxygen increases, Hb saturation increases. In venous blood, pO_2 is 40 mm Hg and Hb is 75% saturated. In arterial blood, pO_2 is 105 mm Hg and Hb is 98% saturated.

> When the partial pressure of O_2 in the plasma is 60 mm Hg, the haemoglobin is 90% saturated. This means that even if the partial pressure of O_2 drops from its normal value of 100% down to 60%, the amount of O_2 carried by the haemoglobin would decrease by only 10%. This provides a safety factor that guarantees a constant supply of oxygen to the tissues. For this reason, certain respiratory and circulatory diseases that result in a lower alveolar ventilation do not have a significant effect on the delivery of oxygen to the tissues.

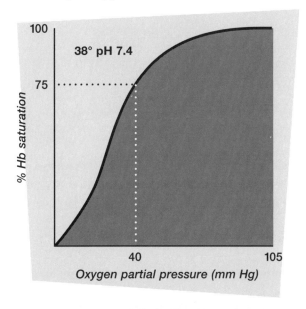

Note: pH = acidity

> As acidity increases, less oxygen combines with Hb.

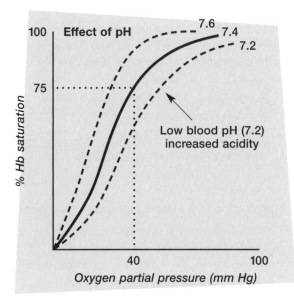

> As temperature increases, less O_2 combines with Hb.

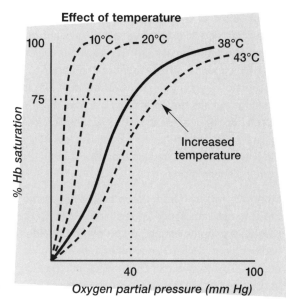

The pO_2 in capillary blood is approximately 40 mm Hg. Thus O_2 diffuses across the alveoli-capillary membrane to equalise concentrations (i.e. pO_2 on both sides of the membrane are identical at 105 mm Hg).

As the blood is then pumped to the tissue sites where O_2 is required to produce energy, a partial pressure gradient occurs between blood at 105 mm Hg and tissue cells at 40 mm Hg. Thus O_2 diffuses into the tissue cells until an equilibrium is achieved when venous blood is at 40 mm Hg. Venous blood returns to the lungs.

Gas transport

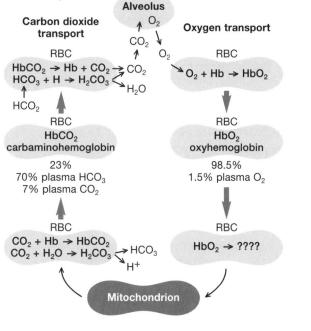

Gas exchange and reactions

> *More about how we use and move oxygen and carbon dioxide.*

More about gas exchange

1 About 98.5% of O_2 is transported by red blood cells combined with haemoglobin. This is known as **oxyhaemoglobin** (HbO_2). The extent to which O_2 + Hb combine is dependent on the partial pressure of oxygen (pO_2). A relatively high pO_2 in the lungs causes greater diffusion across the alveoli capillary membrane. (This has implications for activity at high altitude.) A relatively low pO_2 in the tissue capillaries causes the release of O_2 from the haemoglobin.

2 Most CO_2 released from tissue cells diffuses into the blood stream, then into red blood cells. CO_2 combines with the amino portion of the protein in haemoglobin, whilst O_2 combines with the iron portion. This means that O_2 and CO_2 can be transported simultaneously with no competition.

   In the red blood cells some CO_2 combines with H_2O to form carbonic acid (H_2CO_3) and some combines with haemoglobin to form **carbominohaemoglobin** ($HbCO_2$).

3 About 70% of CO_2 is transported in the blood plasma as **bicarbonate ions** (HCO_3^-). CO_2 is thus transported dissolved in the water of the plasma.

Carbonic anhydrase

This is an enzyme that catalyzes the reaction between CO_2 and H_2O. The resulting H_2CO_3 breaks up, releasing H^- + HCO_3^- ions.

Bicarbonate ions (HCO_3^-) diffuse into blood plasma and are transported to the lungs where the process is reversed, releasing CO_2 to diffuse into lungs.

The Bohr effect

As we have seen, as acidity in the blood increases, haemoglobin releases O_2 more readily. Known as the Bohr effect (see Gas transport diagram – page 21), hydrogen ions exert this effect by combining with Hb and altering its molecular structure.

BPG (bisphosphoglycerate)

This is a substance formed in red blood cells during glycolysis[1]. It binds with haemoglobin, causing it to have a lower affinity with O_2. Glycolysis and BPG production increase when there is an insufficient oxygen supply to the tissues, e.g. during the early stages of intense exercise.

The respiratory system

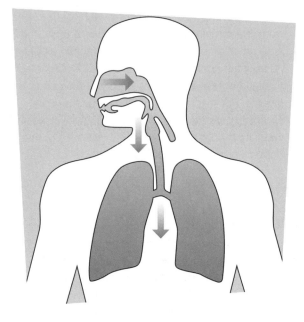

When an athlete breathes it is a complex process. Air travels from the atmosphere outside the body via:

the **nose**, **nasal cavity**, and **mouth** – for warming, filtering and moistening, the …

pharynx – further warming and moistening, the …

larynx – containing the epiglottis which closes during swallowing to prevent food entering the lungs; air passes from the larynx into the …

trachea – a single airway which descends and divides into …

bronchi – which branch into each lung, then further divide into smaller branches, the …

bronchioles and **respiratory bronchioles** – which eventually lead to the …

alveolar ducts – then into the millions of thin-walled …

alveoli – where gas exchange occurs between the respiratory system and the blood (in pulmonary capillaries).

1 A series of reactions in which glucose is converted. The process is anaerobic and represents the first phase in the breakdown of glucose during respiration.

Respiratory volumes

> *Adjusting volumes of air in the lungs.*

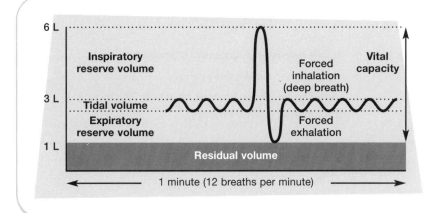

Inspiratory reserve volume = 3100 ml

Vital capacity = 4800 ml

Tidal volume = 500 ml

Total lung capacity = 6000 ml

Expiratory Reserve Volume = 1200 ml

Residual Volume = 1200 ml

Minute Volume – the volume of air inspired or expired in 1 minute: 12 x 500 = 6000 ml/min.

When you are resting, you inhale about 500 millilitres (ml) of air with each breath you take, and exhale about the same amount. You can increase the amount of air taken in by forcing your diaphragm and inspiratory intercostal muscles (see page 18) to expand further than normal. Similarly, you can increase the amount of air exhaled by contracting the intercostal expiratory muscles. Try it for yourself. Breathe in, forcing your ribcage to expand as you do so. Then breathe out, forcing as much air out of your lungs as you can. Repeat this, using the air you exhale to fill up a balloon. How big can you get the balloon with one puff?

> Normally, expiration (breathing out) is a passive activity resulting from the elastic recoil of the lung tissues.

> The amount of air that enters the lungs during a normal, quiet inspiration is about 500 ml; it is called the **tidal volume**. The same volume leaves the lungs during a normal expiration.

> During forced inhalation (a deep breath), the volume of air inspired over and above the tidal volume is called the **inspiratory reserve**. This volume can be as much as 3100 ml. The inspiratory reserve can increase the normal tidal volume 6-fold.

> During forced expiration, the volume of air expired over and above the tidal volume is called the **expiratory reserve**. This volume can be as much as 1200 ml of air. It requires forceful contractions of the intercostal expiratory muscles (internal intercostals, external oblique, rectus abdominis, internal oblique and transversus abdominis).

> Even after the most forceful expiration, some air remains in the lungs. This is called the **residual volume** and equals about 1200 ml. The residual volume prevents the lungs from collapsing. Because residual air remains in the lungs at all times, newly inhaled air is always mixed with air partially depleted of oxygen that is already in the lungs. This prevents the oxygen and carbon dioxide concentrations in the lungs from fluctuating excessively with each breath.

> The vital capacity is the maximum amount of air a person can exhale after taking the deepest breath possible. It is approximately 10-times the volume of air exhaled at rest.

Vital Capacity = Tidal Volume +
Inspiratory Reserve + Expiratory Reserve

4800 ml = 500 ml + 3100 ml + 1200 ml

> The vital capacity plus the residual volume equals the **total lung capacity**, which is about 6000 ml. This total varies with age, sex, and body size.

> Some of the air that enters the respiratory tract during breathing fails to reach the alveoli. This volume (about 150 ml) remains in the conducting portion of the bronchial tree (trachea, bronchi and bronchioles). Since gas exchanges do not occur through the walls of these passageways, this air is said to occupy the 'dead space' (i.e. it is non-functional for gas exchange).

Abilities and skills

> *The foundation of skilled performance.*

Abilities

These are the qualities that you have which make it possible for you to do something.

These abilities underpin the performance of skills.

> Abilities are stable, enduring characteristics.
> They are genetically determined.
> They can be wholly perceptual, wholly motor, or a combination – psychomotor.

Abilities have been classified in the following ways, based on the belief they can be assessed and have relevance to PE:

Muscular power and endurance

Flexibility

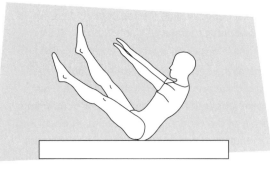

Balance

Co-ordination

Differential relaxation

Other researchers have produced similar lists:

> Explosive strength
> Dynamic strength
> Trunk strength
> Stamina

> Extent flexibility
> Dynamic flexibility
> Gross body equilibrium
> Gross body co-ordination

Others may include:

> Reaction time
> Speed
> Agility

Skills

These are the knowledge and ability that enable you to do something – such as a job, game or sport – very well. Many skills found in a wide range of sports are underpinned by relatively few innate abilities. Talented sports people who appear to be very skilful in a range of sports may be so because they have well-developed abilities which are common to all sports.

> Skills are learnt.

> They are permanent changes in behaviour.

> They have a goal.

> Learning is revealed by changes in consistency of performance, which becomes economic and efficient.

Skills can be wholly perceptual, wholly motor or a combination of both – psychomotor (the ability to process information regarding movements and then put decisions into actions).

Skills have been classified on a variety of continuum (two opposing ends with gradual changes in characteristics between).

Snooker shot	Tennis serve	Shot putt
Fine		*Gross*

Precision of the movement.

Running	Triple jump	Badminton serve
Continuous	*Serial*	*Discrete*

Is there a definite beginning and end?

Tennis serve		Return of tennis serve
Internal pace		*External pace*

Who controls the timing of the movement?

Hockey pass: in game		in practice
Open		*Closed*

Does the environment affect the skill?

Skill learning

If a performer is faced with a particular situation (stimulus) they must find a particular solution (response) to that situation. If the solution works, they are likely to be rewarded and they will do it again.

Coaches like performers to repeat winning or correct solutions. They therefore try to strengthen the connection between the correct response and a particular stimulus.

Some of the many theories associated with the art of learning skills are explained on the next page.

Theories of skill learning

> *How learning takes place.*

Classical conditioning (Pavlov)

This is difficult to show in a sporting context – but situations are set up to connect one response to one stimulus. In sport if the referee blows the whistle, all play stops.

This becomes a conditional response. In training, you practise a drill or routine over and over again so that you will know what to do without really thinking about it – the action becomes conditioned. Can you think of any other examples?

Ivan Pavlov (1849–1936)
Russian physiologist who studied conditional reflexes in animals. At mealtimes, he rang a bell before presenting food to his dogs. After a while, the dogs started salivating whenever they heard the bell, regardless of whether food was presented. This is known as a 'conditional reflex'.

> **Reinforcement** – any action that increases the likelihood of a response occurring again.
> **Positive reinforcement** – reward or praise. The performer is likely to repeat performance in order to be praised again.
> **Negative reinforcement** – removal of praise or reward for incorrect performance. The performer will avoid this response in order not to lose reward.
> **Punishment** – an action that decreases the likelihood of the response occurring again (e.g. 20 press-ups for every basket missed).

Thorndike's Laws

There are three of these:

1 Law of Exercise
Rehearsing the stimulus response (SR) connections is likely to strengthen them. Reinforcement helps.

2 Law of Effect
If the response is followed by a pleasant experience, then the SR bond is strengthened. If it is followed by an unpleasant experience, then the bond is weakened.

3 Law of Readiness
The performer must be mentally and physically competent to perform the task efficiently.

Operant conditioning (Skinner)

This occurs when a performer chooses or achieves the correct response from a range of actions – this is then rewarded by the coach. The performers behaviour is shaped by the coach. The performer need not understand why he or she is performing in this way but only that he or she will be rewarded.

For example, giving a tennis server a particular target to aim for in the court (perhaps half of a service box), then reduce target area to one corner. Rewarding accurate serves strengthens the link.

B.F. Skinner (1904–1990)
American psychologist who studied operant conditioning. This involved looking closely at behaviour patterns developed by reward or punishment. Skinner held that behaviour is shaped and maintained by its consequences.

Trial and error learning

The situation occurs where a range of responses is presented and the performer works through them all until he or she finds the most effective way. This takes time.

An example would be allowing a pupil to discover as many ways as possible of scoring a basket in basketball, then refining the task, asking them to select the most efficient method, e.g. shooting from half-way versus a lay-up shot.

Problem solving (insight learning)

With this idea, learning is based on the intellectual ability of the individual. The person needs to see the whole problem and produce an appropriate solution.

Theories put forward by the **Gestaltists** support this. Learning is based on past experiences.

Feedback

This is the use of information that is available during and after a performance to alter and hopefully improve performance.

Intrinsic feedback

This occurs during the performance. The athlete can feel things in the performance which help them judge the success of the performance. This is also known as continuous feedback or kinaesthesis.

Note: Performers can become dependent on feedback. If feedback is suddenly withdrawn performance may deteriorate particularly if the performer is only doing those actions to receive positive feedback.

Extrinsic feedback

This usually occurs after a performance is completed and is provided by external sources. It is known as terminal feedback or augmented feedback. Extrinsic feedback can be further subdivided into two categories.

a) Knowledge of results (KR)
This is information about the consequences of an action, e.g. did I score a goal or miss? Feedback from a coach about the result, or evidence from a video of performance?

b) Knowledge of performance (KP)
Information about the execution of the action, e.g. coaching points from a coach or a video recording of the action.

This links to the formation of schema especially recognition schema.

Feedback can be...

Motivating

Information about the success of a performance or even a part of a performance can enhance motivation.

E.g. *"You hit all of your forehands today as winners, well done!"*

Failure can also act as a motivator.

E.g. *"You know you can hit better serves than you did today, lets go and work on that in practice."*

COACH

Reinforcing

Thorndike's Law of Effect (refer to page 26) states that rewarded behaviour will be repeated. Rewards may take the form of praise from a coach or from an observed improvement of performance (K.R.).

E.g. *"Great shot. That's exactly what we want."*

COACH

Informational

Feedback that points out errors and provides information to correct those faults.

E.g. *"Ok, but let's work on the angle of approach. Try to come in at a sharper angle."*

COACH

Motor programmes and schema theory

> *Putting thought into action.*

Motor programme theories

These theories deal with how the brain controls movement.

Open loop theory

This explains fast ballistic movements very well. It is concerned with the sending of information or commands.

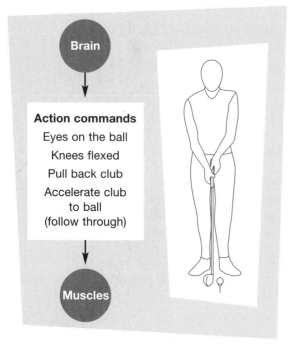

Brain

Action commands
Eyes on the ball
Knees flexed
Pull back club
Accelerate club to ball
(follow through)

Muscles

1 Decision is made in the brain.
2 All information sent in one chunk.
3 Information received by muscles and they perform the action.
4 Feedback may be available but it does not control the action.

> This theory claims we have one motor programme for every action.
> How does the brain store and retrieve these quickly?
> This theory does not account for slow movements where repositioning can take place.

Closed loop theory

This theory explains slow positioning movements very well. Feedback is of prime importance in this theory.

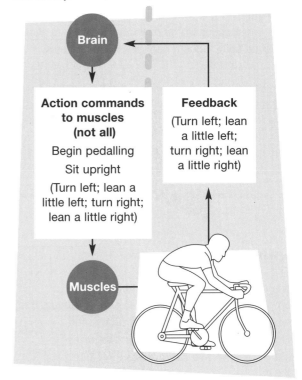

Brain

Action commands to muscles (not all)
Begin pedalling
Sit upright
(Turn left; lean a little left; turn right; lean a little right)

Feedback
(Turn left; lean a little left; turn right; lean a little right)

Muscles

1 Decision made in the brain.
2 Some, but not all, of the information is sent to initiate muscle action.
3 Information is received by the muscles and the movement is initiated.
4 Feedback is available and is used to alter initial movements according to the new needs.

> This theory claims we have one motor programme for each movement.
> How does the brain store and retrieve these quickly?
> Cycling requires constant adjustment of balance. Information comes from feedback to achieve this. How is the motor programme for each new balance stored?

Schema theory

The idea that individual motor programmes contain all the information needed for movement, which are difficult to store and retrieve, was challenged by R.A. Schmidt in 1977.

Schmidt suggested that motor programmes can be clustered and can be adapted to new situations.

The larger the generalised motor programme achieved through variable practice, the more likely it is that it can be adapted to new situations.

A **schema** is all of the information required to make a movement decision. It is stored in long-term memory in the brain.

Recall schema (before movement)

The performer needs to know the following to form a schema.

Initial conditions

1 Where is the:
   > goal
   > opposition
   > team mates?

2 What is the environment like?
   > grass pitch
   > astro turf
   > wet or dry
   > wind directions

3 What condition are they in?
   > fresh
   > tired
   > injured

Response specification

   > How fast do I need to go?
   > How hard shall I pass the ball?
   > Where do I shoot to?
   > Which technique is best?

Recognition schema (after moving)

The performer needs to know the following to correct a response.

Movement outcomes

Knowledge of results
> was it a success?
> was it a failure?

Sensory consequence

Knowledge of performance
> how did it look (extrinsic feedback)?
> how did it feel (intrinsic feedback – kinaesthesis[1])?

1 Kinaesthesis – sense of muscular effort that accompanies a voluntary motion of the body.

Using information

> *The computer brain.*

Processing information

This is how skilled performers make decisions that result in successful and efficient actions:

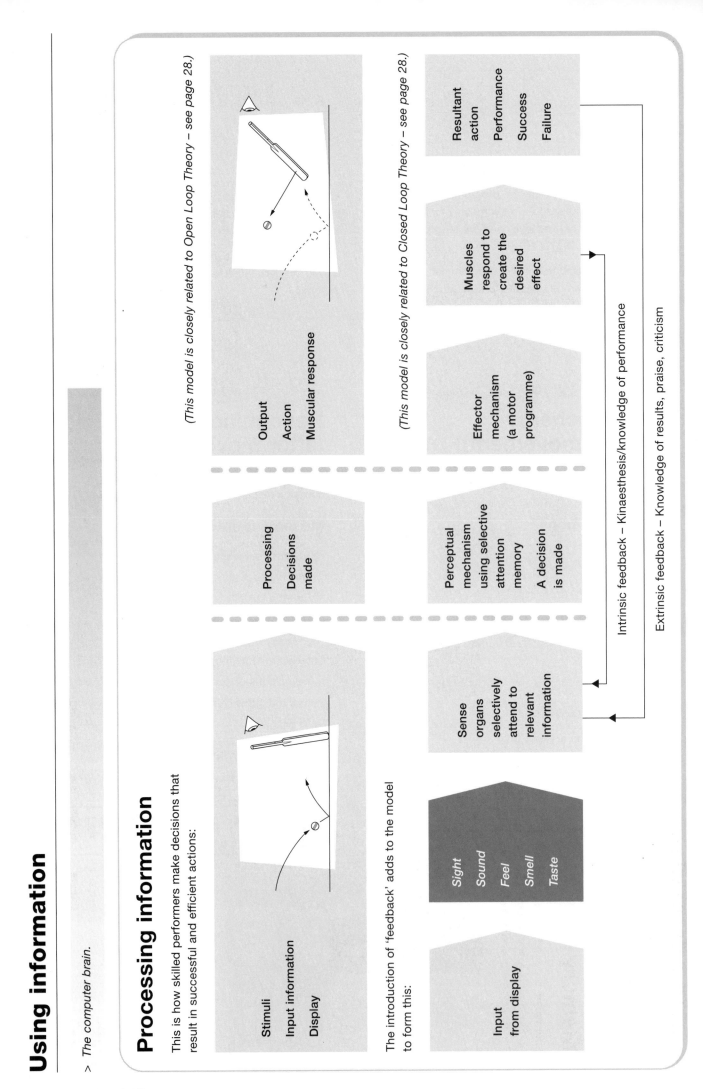

(This model is closely related to Open Loop Theory – see page 28.)

Stimuli
Input information
Display

Processing
Decisions made

Output
Action
Muscular response

The introduction of 'feedback' adds to the model to form this:

(This model is closely related to Closed Loop Theory – see page 28.)

Input from display

Sight
Sound
Feel
Smell
Taste

Sense organs selectively attend to relevant information

Perceptual mechanism using selective attention memory

A decision is made

Effector mechanism (a motor programme)

Muscles respond to create the desired effect

Resultant action
Performance
Success
Failure

Intrinsic feedback – Kinaesthesis/knowledge of performance

Extrinsic feedback – Knowledge of results, praise, criticism

Storing information

> Memories are made of this …

Memory

Information processing is aided by the memory, or experience, of a performer. It is a highly complicated process, but can be represented simply. The processes are not yet fully understood.

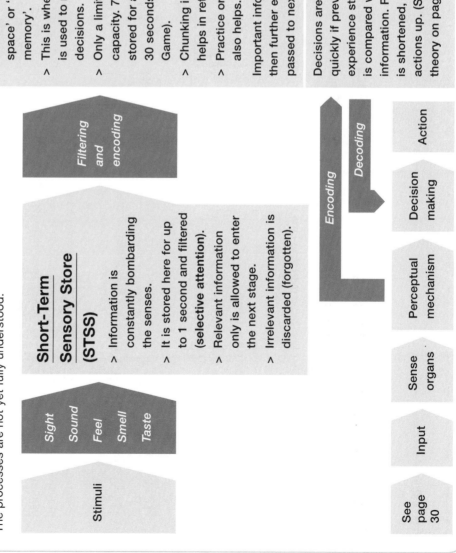

Short-Term Sensory Store (STSS)

> Information is constantly bombarding the senses.
> It is stored here for up to 1 second and filtered (selective attention).
> Relevant information only is allowed to enter the next stage.
> Irrelevant information is discarded (forgotten).

Filtering and encoding

Short-Term Memory (STM)

> Also known as the 'work space' or 'working memory'.
> This is where information is used to make decisions.
> Only a limited storage capacity. 7+/- items stored for approximately 30 seconds (e.g. Kim's Game).
> Chunking information helps in retention.
> Practice or rehearsal also helps.

Important information is then further encoded and passed to next stage.

Decisions are made more quickly if previous experience stored in LTM is compared with current information. Response time is shortened, speeding actions up. (See Schema theory on page 29.)

Encoding
Repetition
Association
Meaningfulness
Novelty

Long-Term Memory (LTM)

This store has a seemingly unlimited capacity and can hold information for a very long time (e.g. 'You never forget how to ride a bike.'). Storage or information is achieved by:

> Repetition (practice) – strengthens motor programmes
> Association – link to already stored information
> Meaningfulness – achieved through understanding the information
> Novelty – Von Restorff Effect

There are thought to be 3 main areas of storage:

1 Procedural – how to do things, motor programmes stored here.
2 Semantic – knowledge (e.g. Paris is the capital of France).
3 Episodic – personal experiences (e.g. 'Last time I did this, this happened and it was successful. I will do it again.').

Decoding

Stimuli — Sight, Sound, Feel, Smell, Taste

See page 30 — Input — Sense organs — *Encoding* — Perceptual mechanism — *Decoding* — Decision making — Action

Responding to information

> *How to do things more quickly.*

Response time (Reaction time)

Information processing is closely linked to a person's ability to make decisions quickly (reaction time) and then transfer them into action (movement time), together known as response time. This is important in all sports.

Response time

The time between the first presentation of stimulus to the movement ending.

Reaction time

The time from the first appearance of the stimulus to the initiation of the first movement. For example, the moment a tennis player is aware of the opponent sending the ball over the net to a particular area of the court, a decision being made to hit a forehand and the first movement to that part of the court.

Movement time

The time taken for the movement, initiated by the stimulus, to begin and then be completed. For example, in tennis the moment that the receiver begins to move into position to hit a forehand shot, including the backswing, until the moment that the player comes back (after impact) into a ready position to prepare for the next shot.

Response time is affected by:

1 Number of stimuli presented – Hick's Law

Time taken to respond (vertical axis)
Number of alternative stimuli (horizontal axis)

2 Age

Reaction time is quicker to an optimum age, then deteriorates.

3 Presentation of stimuli in rapid succession

Psychological refractory period – underpinned by

single-channel hypothesis which is how a fake or dummy works. It takes time for a defender to initiate a response to a fake, which he or she must then stop and restart with their response to the actual movement.

4 Sex

Males have quicker reactions than females, but this also deteriorates more quickly.

5 Stimulus – Response compatibility

If the stimulus was expected, then reaction time will be quicker. If it is not, then reactions will be slower. For example, if a bouncer is bowled in cricket as the last ball of the over then reactions will be quicker than if a slower delivery is bowled.

6 Experience

Using memory to select the correct response speeds up response time.

7 Stimulus intensity

The stronger the stimulus, the faster the reaction, as selective attention is more easily focused on correct stimuli.

8 Anticipation

This can set in readiness the movements required by a stimulus before they are needed – known as spatial anticipation. Predicting an event of a set of stimuli is called temporal anticipation.

Phases of learning

> *Differentiating performers.*

Researchers have identified three phases or stages of learning that all performers go through:

1 **Cognitive or Understanding Phase**
2 **Associative or Verbal Motor Phase**
3 **Autonomous or Motor Phase**

"Learning may be considered to be the more or less permanent change in performance associated with experience." *Knapp (1973)*

"Performance can be seen as the amount of learning that has occurred for the process of learning must be inferred by the observed changes in performance." *Singer (1975)*

Cognitive or Understanding Phase

> Performances in this stage are inconsistent. They lack fluency and success is not guaranteed.
> Attention is all on the skill and cannot be directed elsewhere – relevant cues must be highlighted by the coach.
> Learning occurs through trial and error.
> Correct performances must be reinforced through feedback. Information is best given through demonstration – visual guidance – or through manual guidance, if appropriate.
> "The performer is getting to know what needs to be done."
> Success rate: 2 or 3 out of 10.

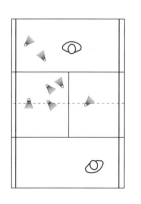

Associative or Verbal Motor Phase

> Performances in this stage are beginning to become more consistent (motor programmes are forming) though still error prone.
> Some of the simpler elements are well learnt; they look fluent; and some of the spare attention is focused elsewhere on more complex or subtle cues and actions.
> The performer can associate their movements with the mental picture they have of the skill.
> Feedback should encourage the performer to 'feel' what a good performance is like – kinaesthesis.
> The performer should begin to detect and correct errors .
> Some never progress beyond this level in some activities.
> Success rate: 5–7 out of 10.

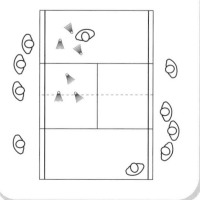

Autonomous or Motor Phase

> Performances in the final stage are skilled, fluent, consistent and aesthetically pleasing.
> Motor programmes are well learnt and stored in long-term memory; therefore reaction time is shorter.
> Skills appear to be automatic as attention is focused elsewhere (e.g. on opponents, tactics, the next move or pass or shot and on employing disguise or fakes to fool the opposition).
> Performers judge their own performances and make changes without external feedback from a coach.
> To remain in this phase constant practice is required to keep reinforcing the motor programmes.
> Success rate: 9 out of 10.

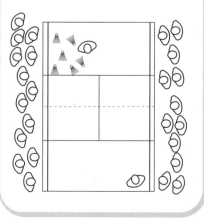

Transfer of skills

> *Using skills in a variety of differing situations.*

This is where the learning, or performance, of one skill influences the learning, or performance, of another skill.

Positive transfer

This occurs when the performance of one skill aids the performance of another skill. It usually occurs when the skills are similar.

"A skilled tennis player may find hitting a smash in badminton is easier because of his ability to serve in tennis."

Coaches can use 'transfer' by ensuring:

> the basic skills are over-learnt, thereby increasing the likelihood of positive transfer

> that the performer understands basic principles common to both sports.

Negative transfer

This occurs when the performance of one skill hinders the performance of another skill.

Negative transfer can occur when a new action is required to a stimulus associated with another skill.

"A squash player who takes up tennis may find the playing of ground strokes difficult initially because in squash a flexible wrist is required, but in tennis a firm wrist is beneficial."

Negative transfer can be avoided:

> if the coach can make the performer aware that transfer is likely

> by ensuring that the practice situation closely resembles the 'match situation' in order to create a large, generalised motor programme.

Proactive transfer

This occurs when skills already learnt affect those to be learnt in the future.

Retroactive transfer

This occurs when skills being learnt now affect those already learnt.

Zero

This form of transfer is experienced when previously learned skills do not affect the learning of new skills.

"Well learned rugby skills are unlikely to affect a person's ability to learn to rock climb."

Researchers have identified six categories of transfer:

1 Transfer between skills (e.g. badminton smash/tennis serve)

2 Practice to performance (e.g. lineout practice at training/same moves used in a match)

3 Abilities linked to skills (e.g. hand-eye coordination/catching in cricket)

4 Limb to limb (bi-lateral) (e.g. hitting tennis shots right handed/hitting tennis shots left handed)

5 Principle to skill (e.g. defensive play in soccer/defensive play in hockey)

6 Stages of learning – skills learned in cognitive phase are built upon in associative phase.

Stimulus generalisation

Is a performer transferring previously learned skills to a new situation in a general way rather than producing a special response to these stimuli?

For example, "A performer learns to catch a ball in cricket. Whenever a ball or object is projected towards that performer they catch it in the same way."

This may not be beneficial as it may not be wise to catch a thrown shot putt, etc.

Response generalisation

Once a specific response is connected to a given stimulus (i.e. well learnt) then the performer begins to adapt the response to vary it. For example, once a forehand return is well learnt the performer will adapt it to the same stimulus by adding spin, cross court, down the line, lob variations.

It's the treble spin, double cross, slam shot, we've been working on.

Teaching – practice and methods

> *The organisation of experiences to ensure an efficient learning situation.*

Teaching

When teaching a skill, guidance is needed from the teacher, coach or friend. There are four elements to the process:

To ensure that pupils learn effectively, a teacher or coach will often manipulate the way in which new skills are demonstrated and then practised. The methods used have advantages and disadvantages depending upon the skills being taught.

1 Instructing

> May be verbal or written, or contained on a worksheet.
> Teacher ensures the pupil understands the task, knows what the targets are and can begin to practise.

2 Demonstrating

> The teacher may perform or it may be appropriate for a peer to demonstrate the skill.
> The pupil must have a model in his/her memory to work from (mental rehearsal). It must be a good demonstration.

4 Confirming

> Need to give intrinsic feedback.
> Need to provide information.
> This is a feedback process. You need to test to find out what the learner has learned. This informs the teacher, helps him/her to set new targets (above) and allows the performer to evaluate his/her performance.

3 Applying

> The pupil must practise the skill in a well-planned situation, that helps him/her to transfer information from practice to a 'real' situation.
> Need to practise skills:
  – opposed   – unopposed
  – whole   – part-whole
  – progressive; part, fixed, massed, variable, distributed.

Types of practice

Fixed practice (drills)

Particularly useful for closed, discrete skills (e.g. basketball free throw). Allows repetition of the performance to strengthen motor programme. Ideally, the skill should be 'over learnt'[1] to allow attention to be focused elsewhere.

[1]Over learning is the practice time spent beyond the time it takes to perfect the skill.

Variable practice

Particularly useful for open skills (e.g. shooting at goal in hockey). Allows repetition of skill but from many different positions and situations. This helps to build up schema to draw upon in a game situation. It can also maintain interest in training and improve motivation.

Massed practice

(No rest intervals between attempts)

Suitable for:
> simple skills (e.g. forehand drives)
> practices designed to simulate fatigued situation late in games
> short training sessions
> the fit learner.

Distributed practice

(rest intervals to mentally rehearse skills)

Most suited to:
> dangerous skills or skills that cause considerable fatigue (e.g. weight training)
> young pupils with short attention spans
> lowly motivated performers
> complex and new skills.

Negative transfer may be a problem!!

Methods

Whole method

The action is demonstrated and then practised as a whole by the pupils. Fast ballistic movements are best taught this way as all parts of the skill interact very closely (e.g. golf swing).

The performer also gets a 'feel' for the skill (kinaesthesis).

Advantages

> Learner appreciates end product.
> Learner gets a feel for the timing.
> Learner understands relationship between subroutines.

Disadvantages

> Unsuitable for complex skills.
> High attention demands; difficult for beginners.
> Not good for dangerous skills.

Part method

The sub-routines of the skill are demonstrated and practised in isolation. Useful if skills are complex with high attention demands, or if skills are dangerous. Success is achieved and motivation maintained. Serial skills are particularly suited to this method. However, transferring learning into whole skill is the key.

Advantages

> Useful for complex skills where performer can cope only with small parts of skill.
> Teacher can focus on specific elements.
> Motivation is maintained through continued success.

Disadvantages

> Transfer from part to whole may not be effective.
> Not useful for highly organised skills.
> Reduces kinaesthetic awareness.
> Lack of continuity.

Whole-part-whole

The whole action is demonstrated and practised. The individual elements are identified and improved before returning skill to whole (e.g. front crawl). Pupil tries whole stroke, weak elements are identified and then practised in isolation (e.g. using a float to practise leg kick).

If skill is very complex 'mini skills' can be taught (e.g. mini tennis instead of full game).

Advantages

> Performer gets a feel for whole skill then practises elements of it.
> Success is continual if weak elements are practised.
> Practices can be focused very carefully.

Disadvantages

> Transfer from part to whole may be difficult.

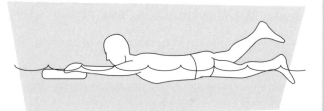

Progressive part method

Also known as **chaining method**. Skill is broken into sub-routines, which are practised in isolation and well learnt.

Part one is well learnt, so is part two; then the two are joined together; part three is then learned in isolation and then added to parts one and two. Particularly effective for serial skills (e.g. gymnastics sequences or triple jump).

Advantages

> Weaknesses are targeted, then practised and improved.
> Performer understands the relationships of sub-routines.

Disadvantages

> Takes time to get to full skill.

Teaching – styles and guidance

> *The organisation of experience to ensure an efficient learning situation.*

Teaching styles

This is the way a coach or teacher decides to handle the learning situation.

The method chosen will depend upon:

> the teacher's personality and ability

> the activity being taught – more dangerous activities will need a more authoritarian approach

> learner's ability – beginner may need more teacher input than more experienced pupils

> pupils' motivation

> age range of pupils

> learning environment.

Mosston and Ashworth spectrum of styles

Based on observed PE lessons but applicable to all teaching. Mosston and Ashworth, 1986.

They characterised styles by the degree of decision making by teacher and pupils.

Teacher decision	
	Pupil decision

Styles of teaching

A   B   C   D   E   F   G   H   I   J

Styles A + B are characterised by lots of teacher-made decisions (e.g. command style, practice style). All learners do the same thing.

Styles C + D have the pupils making some decisions about what they do (e.g. reciprocal style).

All learners following the same basic progressions but with some ability to change practices.

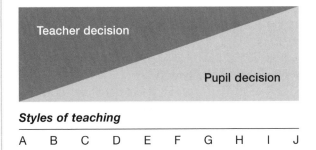

Styles E + F + G are democratic styles involving negotiation between teacher and pupils (e.g. self-check, guided discovery style).

Styles H + I + J are pupil-centred discovery styles where pupils make most of the decisions: (e.g. problem solving, discovery style).

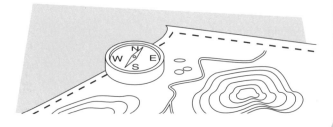

Guidance

The way in which a teacher transmits information to the learner. Learners receive information using all their senses, so a combination of approaches is usually best.

Visual guidance

Demonstration – to help create a mental picture of skill. This is closely linked to Albert Bandura's 1977 research on modelling. The 'model' must be as close to perfect as possible as the learner has to imitate it. It must be realistic (e.g. do not try to teach pupils who are around 157 cm tall to slam dunk).

Often used in conjunction with verbal guidance to highlight key points.

Visual aids:
photographs, charts and diagrams tend to be too static. Video playback in slow motion can be very effective.

Modification of display:
teacher enhances the perception of the pupil by highlighting particular aspects of the surroundings (e.g. coloured targets on court to aim at; fluorescent golf balls).

Verbal guidance

Often linked with demonstration. Not so useful by itself.

Points to note:
> Does the performer understand the language being used?
> Can the performer remember everything that has been said?
> Can the performer translate instructions into actions?

Verbal guidance highlights cues (e.g. 'Wave goodbye to the ball' when shooting in basketball; 'Clean palm, dirty neck' in shot putt).

Manual guidance

Physical restriction – a person, or more commonly an object, confines the movement of the learner (e.g. 'somersault belt' in trampoline; a 'tight rope' in climbing; 'waterwings' on a young swimmer).

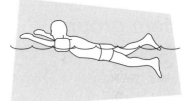

> Gives the performer confidence.
> Helps to increase safety in dangerous situations.
> Allows the performer to work out timings of the skill.

Forced response:
The performer is guided manually through the shot to be learned (e.g. badminton short serve – the teacher extends the arm by pushing on the elbow of the player).
> Gives a supported kinaesthetic feel for the shot. If overused the performer may become dependent on help or may lose motivation as they are a passive learner.

Key ideas – key definitions

> *Our field of study outlining issues and concepts.*

Historical

What was it like in the past?

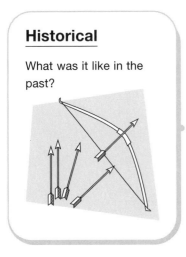

A contemporary socio-cultural view

The performer in society.

We must:
> consider issues that arise...
- excellence
- discrimination
- mass participation
- outdoor recreation
> think about other perspectives of the activity and performer...

Comparative

What is it like in other countries?

> Globalisation

Classification of activities

Within our field of study, physical performance can be classified into **five main groups** with unique features.

Main groups

1 Combat
(e.g. fencing)

involves beating an opponent in a stylized war game

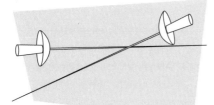

2 Outdoor pursuits/conquest
(e.g. sailing)

challenge against nature or with a physical/psychological objective

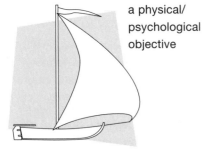

3 Aesthetic
(e.g. gymnastics)

visual, competition criteria

4 Individual
(e.g. swimming)

athletic, aquatic, competing on own, physical challenge, self-fulfilling, recreation, physical education or sport

5 Games

contrived structured competitive experiences, existing in own time and space, can be partner or team

> **Invasion**
(e.g. hockey)

attack by entering an opponent's territory to score in their goal

> **Target/striking**
(e.g. cricket)

hit to score, opposition field to limit scoring

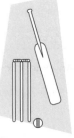

> **Court**
(e.g. tennis)

non contact, score in opponent's court area

When studying socio-cultural issues we must consider three questions:

1 What do we mean by...?

> This deals with definitions.

2 How do we know?

> Here we need to consider authoritative back-up.

3 What does this tell us?

> The influence of the past on what it is like now.

Main concepts

We can also see **four main categories** or **concepts**. Most activities can exist in each category depending on the attitude of the performer and the level and organisation of the performance. Thus, as examples, football or swimming, can be undertaken for:

> play
> physical recreation
> sport, or
> physical education.

These concepts have some shared characteristics:

> improved health
> personal development
> challenge or competition
> physical endeavour.

1 Play

spontaneous, often child-like, physical activity

2 Physical recreation

physical activity with limited organisational structure

3 Physical education

formal learning of knowledge and values through physical activities

4 Sport

structured physical activity requiring a high degree of commitment

Intrinsic

An experience complete in itself.

Within society the *performer* is influenced by:

> what the activity is
> why they are doing it
> how they are doing it
> where they are doing it
> with whom they are doing it
> for whom they are performing.

Physical performance is a dynamic experience

The physical experience may be **intrinsic** or have **extrinsic** factors.

Extrinsic

The main extrinsic factors which influence the *physical situation* are:

> geographical location
> social
> political
> economic.

These factors can be influenced by local, regional, national and international influence.

Concepts of physical activity

> *The characteristics of the concepts of play, physical recreation, physical education and sport. Activities can be placed on the continuum from play to sport.*

> ## Unorganised
> ('Paidia' – child's fun)
> **play**

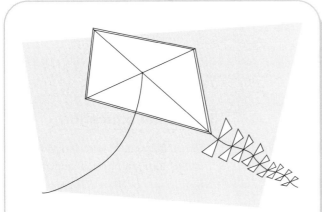

Play

Characteristics

> enjoyable

> spontaneous, voluntary

> without pre-determined rules

> child-like

> intrinsic

> self-fulfilling

> time and space – may be limited and may be changed by agreement

Refer to classical theories of play – Huizinga, Piaget, Callois and Ellis. It has been suggested that all sports have their origin in play. Callois suggested that play is a **reflection of society**.

Features of play

> biological – instinctual part of learning process in developing skills

> psychological – learning about self

> sociological – to practise social roles

> children play – to learn about life

> adults play – to escape the stresses of everyday life

"to play" – do the activity

"fair play" – the morality of sport

Physical recreation

Can be considered as 'constructive or active **LEISURE**' taken in the time left after work, duty and bodily needs have been met. This implies there is an **economic factor**.

Characteristics of physical recreation

> relaxation (physical recovery)

> recuperation (recover from stress)

> recreation (be creative)

> time and space decided by participant

> limited organisation

> participant chooses

> intrinsic rewards

> physical enjoyment

> spiritual well-being

> social

> mental pleasure

> non-productive

Outdoor recreation

> in the natural environment

> can be physically challenging but not necessarily competitive

Organised

('Ludus' – organised sport)

display

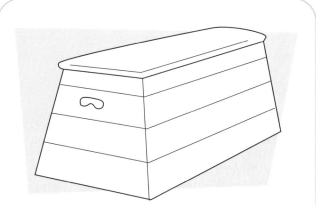

Physical education

Features of physical education

> to impart knowledge and values through physical activities concerning bodily movement

> usually in an institution

> structured lessons

> develops practical skills to be able to participate in activities

> develops social skills to work with others as part of a team, develop co-operation and leadership

> develop lifestyle activities

> extra curricular activities out of formal lesson times

> national curriculum for PE to bring uniformity

> examinations (GCSE, A-level, degree) raised the profile of PE and encouraged career development

> develops values – social, instrumental, humanistic

Outdoor education

> using the environment as a resource for learning physical activities

> challenges self

> develops awareness and respect for the environment

> learn to work with and depend on others

> provides sense of danger/adventure

Sport

Features of sport

> competitive

> highly organised

> time and space designated

> formal rules

> requires higher level of skill

> develop sportsmanship

> requires commitment

> intrinsic rewards (own achievement, satisfaction)

> extrinsic rewards (cups, money, titles, etc.)

> the 'letter' of playing the game – by the rules

> the 'spirit' of playing the game – fair play, high morals

can be functional or dysfunctional
(Refer to Nash's model)

functional – high – played in the spirit of the game – abide by the rules, even if no referee decision given

dysfunctional – low – breaking of rules, aggression towards others, 'sending off'

Sport and culture

> Sport exists in all societies, past and present. We can look at how it is used by developing countries.

> **Society** is a community of people coming together and relating to each other.
> **Culture** is a product of this relationship – often represented by a society's customs, religion, art, etc.
> **Sport** is a part of culture... and a reflection of society.

Sport exists within society and is a part of social life.

It reflects the ideas and beliefs of the community which draws up its rules and laws and defines acceptable behaviour.

Looking at different societies in historical context we see how sports developed through the needs of the culture and society.

Ancient societies

(those civilisations that don't exist today)

Ideology – suited to their beliefs

Evidence of sports pursued by ancient societies show a relationship between ideology of the civilisation and the sports pursued.

Functional

Some sports had a functional basis:
> keeping soldiers fit for defence
> practising the skills of hunting
> keeping the masses occupied
  e.g. slaves watching Roman gladiators.

Ritual

Other sports were related to ritual:
> symbolic of life stages
> representing religious beliefs
> a ceremony or festival.

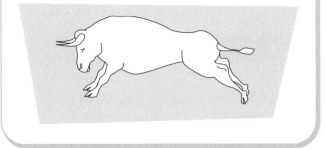

Tribal societies

(those that are lacking in sophistication, often with a 'primitive' god/man belief)

Ritual

> sports may reflect the relationship between god and man and could be used as a ritual to appease the Gods
> in ball games the ball may have represented the sun
> in some cases the heads of defeated enemies were used as the ball in a display of victory and strength
> tests of strength such as wrestling matches were used to prepare warriors or elect chiefs.

Survival

> some sports such as running and spear throwing were physical preparation for basic survival (Zulus and Indians)
> skills needed to be learnt for finding food and defence.

Natural

> learning how to adapt within the natural environment.

Some rituals survived colonisation. After colonisation sports were **ADAPTED** or **ADOPTED** by countries.

Emergent societies

(countries that are less developed economically and have a low level of technology – largely found in Africa, the Far East and South America)

Sport is often used as a means to achieve political strategies and develop emergent countries. Sport is an area where emergent societies can emulate and compete with advanced societies.

Sport can be used as a method of creating **STABILITY** by means of:

Nation building

> increasing internal national identity
> increasing **international identity** – sport as a 'shop window' for a society
> facilitating international representation.

Integration

> encouraging multi-ethnic sporting activities and **relieving racial tensions**
> bringing the nation together to support an individual or team and so **appeasing the population** and **diverting attention** from other problems.

Health

> mass participation is encouraged to develop a more health conscious society
> increased general health produces a fit fighting force.

Defence

> creating a high profile defence to protect the country
> the military is often the organiser of sport and creates opportunities to participate.

Some emerging nations have striven for excellence in a limited range of sports, channelling money into a small elite. This may bring attention to the country and set up the champions as role models. However the disproportionate funding of one sport to achieve excellence may be at the expense of other goals (e.g. overcoming poverty).

Examples of what sport... and why?

Initially, emergent countries tend to use one dominant sport. Once established, the country can develop other sports.

Indonesia – badminton

> minority sport which suits country
> Olympic sport – thus seen by the world
> easy to administer
> non-contact – non-aggressive
> small-sided game – small population
> requires small physical stature, dexterity and quick reactions
> little equipment or space needed
> slow pace – and ideal for playing in the tropics.

The West Indies – cricket

> traditional and established game
> brought islands and races together in common purpose
> team game – co-operation
> outdoor game – healthy
> Commonwealth sport – able to play other nations
> international reputation
> income to islands.

Kenya – middle and long distance running

> Olympic sport – high profile
> suited to lifestyle – used to running long distances
> little expense or technical knowledge needed
> good training at altitude
> a few athletes can create great national pride.

Political models

> *How countries use sport will depend on their political model.*

Do political models affect a nation's approach to sport? Yes.

Authoritarian and one-party states – the socialist model

Communist states (China) and the old eastern European socialist countries use sport as a political tool.

What are the common driving forces?

Political

Sport and politics are linked, politics controlling and using sport. The government exercises centralised control over sport. The person is not as important as the political ideal. The state is seen as benevolent and promotes collectivism – all working together to achieve same goal.

Excellence

Excellence is also a political tool since sporting success equals political success. There is the 'shop window' effect; the country shows the rest of the world only what it wants to be seen. Sporting success, seen by the world, would suggest the political model is a success.

Functional

Recreation and sport are not primarily for self-fulfilment but function as a vehicle of the state. They may inspire or appease the population.

Egalitarianism

Equal opportunity is preached although often the talented are given privileges at the expense of the ordinary person. This is justified by the state to achieve role models for international exposure to promote the country's status.

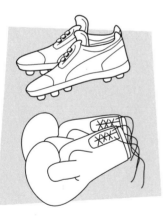

Sport and humanistic values

Sport can be an experience or an entertainment (i.e. TV Gladiators) and (especially in developed democracies) will reflect elements of society such as social, economic or racial groupings.

Mass (or low) culture

> The working class or ordinary people create sporting traditions and identity – these exist where differences in status, race, wealth are strong.

> An individual can lose their identity in a collective identity – there is a common bond where sport has brought them together.

> The identity issue may lead to keen rivalry which can cause crowd reaction to an event or decision – a home crowd 'defend' its home ground.

> Over excitement (initiated from within the group or from a situation outside the group) may cause unacceptable or unlawful crowd behaviour when emotions run high – football hooliganism in the UK often involves young working class males.

> Some may use this for dysfunctional behaviour – anti-social or aggressive – with resultant crime and police and media attention.

> Within the sport the physical involvement will be within the rules. In boxing, violence is acceptable in the ring but not outside it. Football players must stay within the rules or be carded or dismissed for breaking them.

Multi-party democracies – the capitalist model

In multi-party democracies sport is primarily an economic function. The organisation of sport is devolved and each person is treated as an individual. We can see a pattern within the modern industrialised G7 countries (those with high technology and economic wealth) Canada, the USA, the UK, Italy, Germany, France and Japan.

What are the driving forces?

Nationalism

Nationalism is strong and sport is used as a symbol of national identity and a vehicle to promote it. The UK still divides itself for some sport (six nations rugby). France is recognised for the Tour de France, USA for American football.

Excellence

Sport is an arena where individuals can achieve optimum potential, seen through their own performance or the commercial value. The 'rags to riches' stories of athletes provide hope for all (including minorities) and the belief that anyone can achieve the 'American dream' of success, wealth and status... and therefore happiness?

Recreational

Sports are an escape from work and duty. Leisure time is available for all for recreation in advanced sophisticated and wealthy societies. Sport can be experienced as a participant or spectator and is seen as character building and re-creative.

Commercial

Sport is seen as a commodity and if the commodity is scarce (e.g. a highly skilled performer) it becomes valuable. The commodity is bought and sold and becomes big business and it can be used to sell products. There are other aspects of commercialism: advertising and sponsorships, media involvement and the sale of equipment, memberships, ground admissions, etc.

High culture

> Sport is enjoyed for its own sake and seen as intellectual and civilising.

> Sport may be high in social status, especially where it is exclusive (elitist) and expensive.

> Artistic and aesthetic values may be important; some activities are an art form, with qualities as judged by a panel.

> Performing arts/sports such as gymnastics and dance allows the individual to test their own skill. Several of the more expressive sports are female dominated.

> High moral values can be attached to sport – self fulfilling and raises awareness of self and refinement of the mind. Intrinsic.

> Audience (not always called the 'crowd') behaviour is civilised and knowledgeable; spectators can share in an intellectual and aesthetic experience

> Sport is a meeting of mind, body and spirit.

Physical education, sport and sub-cultures

> *Inequalities exist in physical education and sport. Minority groups are often disadvantaged; we can look at this in terms of opportunity, provision and esteem.*

Inequalities still occur in advanced western societies and are reflected in sport, often due to cultural and historical influences.

One section of the community – minority groups – may be disadvantaged and discriminated against in physical education and sport. Also damaging is the fact that sports myths and stereotypes have developed around minority groups.

Opportunity

Race

> parental expectations
> non-acceptance in clubs may be a barrier
> may be affected by religious beliefs (e.g. muslim girls)
> lack of finance means little choice (many low paid)
> cultures may not rate PE and sport highly
> 'staking' – assumption that you play in a particular position in the team ('brawn not brain' stereotype)
> lack of career opportunities – majority of coaches (and the decision makers) are white

Disability

> some sports may not cater for disability – therefore restricted choice of activities
> few disabled sports clubs and restricted membership to others
> few disabled coaches so poor career prospects
> overall, fewer opportunities to achieve excellence

Gender

> looking after family – less leisure time
> certain religious restrictions
> fewer female coaches, managers and administrators therefore limited career opportunities
> some clubs have membership restrictions – although law is changing
> lack of competition opportunity
> restricted choice of activities and those choices may favour males – school, National Curriculum (team game bias)
> considered incapable and not aggressive enough for coaching

Age

> young – too early with hard training can 'burn out'
> young – reliant on parental attitude and finances
> participation of 50+ age group restricted, few veterans' clubs and teams
> age restrictions in some clubs
> curriculum and extra curricular opportunities dependent on schools – relies on PE staff enthusiasm

Class

> 'working class' – little leisure time, lack of finance, difficult to work and compete at a high level
> restricted access to certain clubs
> 'middle class' – more leisure time and wealth to choose activities

Provision

- > associated with a particular sport, e.g. Asians playing cricket and Afro Caribbean youths boxing... therefore little provision in other sports
- > lack of single sex lessons
- > lack of changing facilities to cater for religious restrictions
- > information not easily available
- > coaches not available

- > lack of specialised equipment
- > poor wheelchair access to leisure centres and swimming pools
- > inadequate changing facilities
- > few activities provided at leisure centres
- > transport to activities may not be possible
- > cost of special provision may be prohibitive

- > lack of creche facilities
- > few females on governing bodies and little input in decision-making
- > few female coaches
- > lower pay and prize money
- > may lack money to spend on sport if not working
- > lack of transport
- > competitions may be restricted to single sex
- > clubs may restrict playing times or provide inferior changing facilities

- > facilities dependant on geographical location
- > few activity sessions specifically for older people or teenagers
- > transport may be reliant on goodwill of family and friends
- > fees may be prohibitive

- > 'working class' may experience limited facilities and coaches – reliant on sponsorship for funding
- > wealthy individuals have the ability to pay a coach, buy equipment and clothing and to travel to training and competition

Esteem

- > lack of role models to give hope to achieve
- > poorly paid or menial job add to low self esteem
- > lack of coaches from same ethnic group
- > media coverage of indigenous sports is low

- > perceived to be not able to achieve and the assumption that they cannot do sport – a myth and stereotype
- > few role models – paraplegic games and marathons poorly covered
- > assumed lack of knowledge
- > perceived as not interesting or exciting enough for media coverage, spectators or sponsorship... therefore not taken seriously

- > think they can't do sport – poor self image
- > lack of many role models
- > media coverage poor, tends to focus on appearance instead of skill and ability – only for show portraying traditional gender role ideology (mostly golf, tennis and athletics covered)
- > lack of sponsorship as competition considered not as exciting as males
- > not taken seriously by spectators – considered recreational
- > affected by myths – girls can't throw effectively, women will damage themselves in certain events or are not able to do others

- > media coverage minimal for both elderly and very young
- > few role models
- > elderly perceived as only involved for recreation
- > peer pressure can affect youngsters perception of sport, particularly girls

- > role models can give hope to those from deprived backgrounds – seen as way out and means to achieve wealth
- > media can help promote and gain sponsorship
- > less wealthy could be seen as less able or knowledgeable

Current and recent issues in sport

> *Issues in sport, excellence, mass participation, professionalism, drugs.*

Sport is often in the news and on the political and social agenda – sometimes because of governmental initiatives which result from social pressures.

There are particular issues which will affect how sport is played and developed.

Excellence

Excellence is important as it suggests economic success. The government's 'Raising the Game' initiative (1995) aimed to develop sport in the UK from school to Olympic level. More recently:

> The Sportsmark Scheme – recognition of best schools.
> Sports Schools – opportunities for excellence.
> UK Institute of Sport – centre of excellence.

excellence

performance

participation

foundation

One (widely held) belief is that a broad base gives the best chance for people to achieve excellence.

Opportunity must be accessible to all who have the ability and desire – they will have the best chance of succeeding. Need to ensure those with promising ability get to the top. Not everyone can or will achieve but all should have the opportunity to try at foundation level.

Only the few – the elite – will achieve excellence. How elite depends on the base. Advanced societies can afford to have a wider base – emergent countries start with a single sport and then widen the base by developing others.

What influences the activities chosen at foundation level?
> had to (on school curriculum)
> parents did it and encouraged
> tradition within social group
> other persuasive factors (e.g. media, advertising)

A broad base gives the opportunity to experience a wide variety of activities. This permits an informed choice – if you don't try, you don't know. In order to develop sports talent you need to select and develop talent and support performance.

To achieve excellence you need:
> coaching
> facilities
> competition
> training
> funding for equipment training
> sports science input

Mass participation

Encouraging everyone to play

A landmark government initiative was 'Sport for All' (1972). The aim was to increase participation by all people regardless of sex, age, race or class, with particular emphasis on groups with low participation:
> disabled
> post-16
> women
> 50 years plus
> unemployed.

Everybody encouraged to participate in physical activity either at recreational or sporting level. The take up of sport is heavily dependent on opportunity, provision and esteem (see pages 52–53).

Encouragement given to:
> pre-school children – top tots, top start
> school children – top play, top sport, National Curriculum, extra curricular, top link
> adolescents – in schools and clubs
> adults – leisure centres, access to more clubs and competitions
> elderly – off peak facilities, veterans clubs and teams and promotion of lifetime sports

Professionalism

What changes when a sport moves from amateurism to professionalism.

> professionalism is equated with top level competition and extrinsic rewards – cups, titles, payment: amateurism – physical recreation
> there is a need for good organisation and consistent rules, structures developed by the governing bodies
> results become more important
> increased pressure on those involved
> increased amount and quality of training
> a high degree of skill is required
> better facilities and funding
> attracts spectators, media coverage and sponsorship

What about drugs in sport?

Athletes take performance-enhancing drugs to help them achieve. All such drugs are banned by the International Olympic Committee... and all other significant ruling bodies.

> stimulants – increase alertness and reduce pain and fatigue
> narcotics – kill pain
> anabolic steroids – build muscle bulk
> diuretics – speed weight loss by increasing the amount of water excreted
> blood doping – increases amount of oxygen in the body

The gold medal and the desire to be the best are driving forces.

Drugs are banned. They are seen as cheating. Drugs represent:

> an illegal act
> a poor win ethic
> a health risk
> a poor role model.

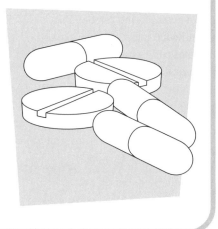

Who pays?

> public
  – government
  – local government
  – lottery
> voluntary
  – private clubs
  – subscriptions
  – governing bodies
> private
  – sponsorship
  – tv and radio companies
  – companies
  – individuals

Who controls sports in the UK?

Agencies and administration

Many QUANGOs (quasi-autonomous non-governmental organisations) with money from central government but run independently... although the government will still exercise considerable influence.

Sports Council (1972) (now Sport England)
Fund and run centres of excellence and the new Institute of Sport. Encourages all to participate in sport and PE. Responsible for National Sports Centres and also for distributing the money that sport receives through the National Lottery. The Sports Council works closely with the Central Council for Physical Recreation.

The Central Council for Physical Recreation (1935)
The CCPR is the umbrella organisation that represents more than 250 governing bodies of individual sports. It is largely a pressure group, encouraging participation and working on behalf of sports.

National Coaching Foundation (1983)
Set up by the Sports Council; it's primary focus is on developing excellence through the improvement of coaching techniques. Much of its work is in coaching the coaches, but also does work directly with young performers.

British Olympic Association (1904)
The BOA organises and co-ordinates British participation in the Olympics.

Youth Sports Trust (1994)
To provide all children in the UK with an introduction to sport and the means to progress.

Countryside Agency (Countryside Commission)
Responsible for National Parks and co-ordinates with many outdoor pursuits organisations.

Forestry Commission of Great Britain
Responsible for forests and woodlands which include many centres for walking, orienteering, cycling, etc.

Also central and local government
Minister for Sport (part of the Department of National Heritage, created in 1960)
Local Authorities

And other organisations such as...

Sports aid Foundation (1976)
Self financing body mainly for funding top amateurs.

Individual sports governing bodies
Administering the sports (often rules, competitions, national team, etc.).

Energy concepts

At any one time enormous numbers of chemical reactions are taking place inside a human cell. These reactions either require energy or are releasing it.

Definitions

Energy: A physical quantity that measures the capacity of a system for doing work. In other words, your capacity to perform work.
Symbol: *E*;
units: Calories or Joules
(1 cal = 4.2 Joules)

Work: A transfer of energy as a consequence of a force acting through a distance.
Work = Force x Distance
Symbol: *W*; unit: Joule (J)

Power: The rate of transfer of energy between one system and another. Measured as work performed per unit of time.
Symbol: *P*; unit: Watt
(Joules per second)

$$\frac{\text{Work}}{\text{Time}}$$

Exothermic reaction: reaction that releases energy.

Endothermic reaction: reaction that requires an input of energy.

Enzyme: biological catalyst that brings about and speeds up specific reactions.

Metabolism: the sum of all chemical reactions in the body.

Anabolic: building up.

Catabolic: breaking down.

Basal metabolic rate (BMR): the rate (minimum energy) at which the chemical processes of the body must function in order to sustain life. Affected by: age, sex, occupation, metabolism.

Energy efficiency

To evaluate the relationship between input (energy expenditure) and resulting mechanical output in exercise, we need to assess the mechanical efficiency of human movement.

$$\% \text{ Efficiency} = \frac{\text{Useful work done}}{\text{Energy expenditure}} \times 100$$

Human range = 12–25%

For every movement made only 25% of energy consumed contributes directly to actual movement, the rest is converted into HEAT.

Note: Improvement in techniques used and overall skill levels will increase efficiency of energy used.

Respiratory exchange ratio (RER or RQ) – used to estimate energy expenditure per litre of O_2 used.

$$RER = \frac{\text{Amount of } CO_2 \text{ produced}}{\text{Amount of } O_2 \text{ used}}$$

Fats = 0.70
Protein = 0.80
Carbohydrates = 1.0
Mixture of fats and carbohydrates = 0.85

Used to estimate proportion of fats and carbohydrates being oxidised.

Forms of energy in the body

Energy in (pod) =
Energy out (work) + (heat)
Energy stored (fat)

Laws of thermodynamics

(transformation of energy by heat and work)

First Law: Energy is not destroyed or lost but passed from one form to another.

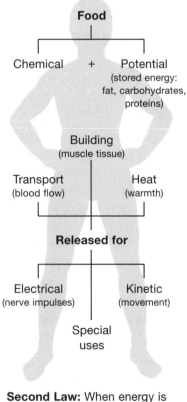

Food

Chemical + Potential
(stored energy: fat, carbohydrates, proteins)

Building
(muscle tissue)

Transport
(blood flow)

Heat
(warmth)

Released for

Electrical
(nerve impulses)

Kinetic
(movement)

Special uses

Second Law: When energy is exchanged, the efficiency of exchange is imperfect, and part of the energy will escape as heat.

Applying energy concepts

> *Applying energy concepts to performance.*

Constructing a training programme

> You must consider the specific energy demands of the particular sport.
> Training must mirror the demands of the sport by stressing the appropriate energy system used.

Nutrition and performance

> The right foods in right amounts at the right times can make a significant difference to a performance.
> Analysing energy expenditure of a particular activity can give valuable information on how much energy is required.

Warm up/ cool down

> It is important to do light exercise immediately before and after playing sport or doing strenuous activity.
> Increases body and muscle temperature.
> Increases enzyme activity in the metabolic reactions found in the energy systems.
> Increases blood flow by keeping capillary beds open in muscles to aid oxygen transport.

Control of body weight

> Understanding energy expenditure and energy imput will help you to maintain a constant body weight.

Input < Output
(lose weight)

Input = Output
(maintain weight)

Input > Output
(gain weight)

Maintenance of body temperature

> A large proportion of energy produced is in the form of heat.
> Understanding how heat is lost or gained through convection, conduction, radiation and evaporation will help keep your body temperature constant at 37°C.

Fatigue

> Understanding how energy is produced within the body will provide a valuable insight into what fatigue is.
> It will also show how fatigue can be reduced, or even avoided, during performance.

ATP – the energy currency

> The body's energy wage.

Adenosine triphosphate (ATP)

ATP is the main supplier of metabolic energy in living cells. It is a high-energy compound that is central to all that takes place during metabolism.

This part of the molecule acts like a 'handle'. Its shape can be recognised by highly specific enxymes.

This part of the molecule contains bonds (O–P) which can be hydrolysed (broken down by water) in reactions which are *exergonic* (energy yeilding) and can be coupled to *endergonic* (energy-demanding) reactions.

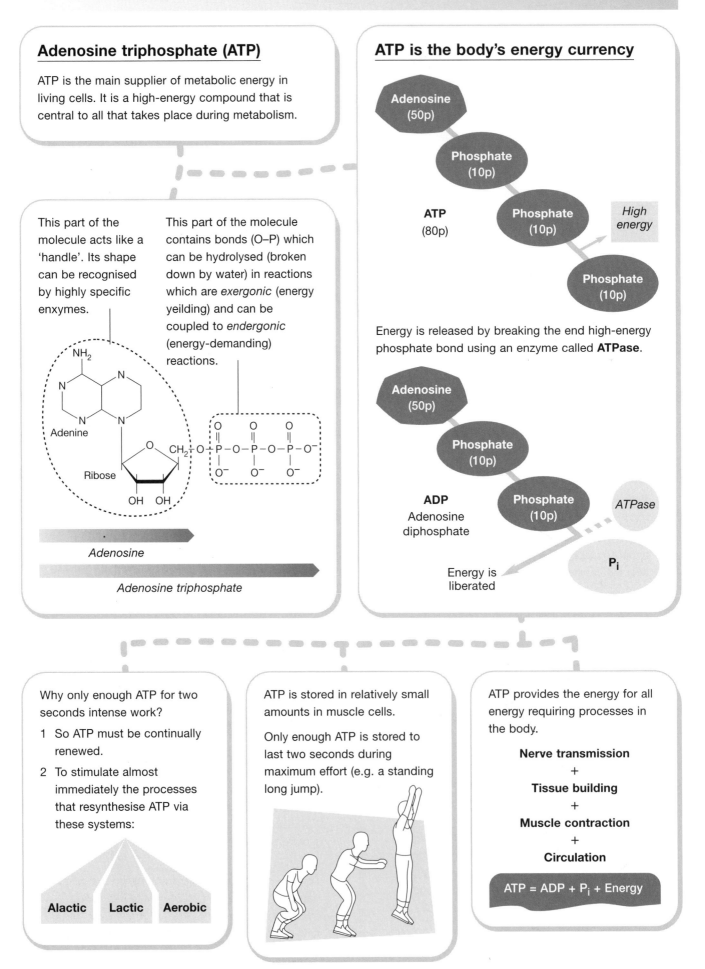

Adenine

Ribose

Adenosine

Adenosine triphosphate

ATP is the body's energy currency

Adenosine (50p)

Phosphate (10p)

ATP (80p)

Phosphate (10p)

High energy

Phosphate (10p)

Energy is released by breaking the end high-energy phosphate bond using an enzyme called **ATPase**.

Adenosine (50p)

Phosphate (10p)

ADP
Adenosine diphosphate

Phosphate (10p)

ATPase

P_i

Energy is liberated

Why only enough ATP for two seconds intense work?

1. So ATP must be continually renewed.

2. To stimulate almost immediately the processes that resynthesise ATP via these systems:

Alactic **Lactic** **Aerobic**

ATP is stored in relatively small amounts in muscle cells.

Only enough ATP is stored to last two seconds during maximum effort (e.g. a standing long jump).

ATP provides the energy for all energy requiring processes in the body.

Nerve transmission
+
Tissue building
+
Muscle contraction
+
Circulation

ATP = ADP + P_i + Energy

The recovery process (1)

> *Paying back the energy currency spent.*

Resynthesis of ATP during and after exercise

We need ATP constantly and cannot afford to run out of it. Three sources of energy replacement ensure ATP is always available.

3 The aerobic system *overleaf*

1 ATP/PC system:
Phosphocreatine system
Alactacid system

As maximal exercise begins, e.g. 100 m sprint/long jump, ATP stored in the muscles breaks down to ADP and energy is released. Increasing concentrations of ADP in the sacroplasm stimulates the release of the enzyme.

Creatine Kinase

This substance initiates the breakdown of **phosphocreatine** and energy is released from the bond between creatine and phosphate.

The energy released reforms the bonds between ADP and the phosphate available in the sacroplasm to form ATP, which is subsequently broken down to release energy for muscular contractions.

Phosphocreatine is a simple compound easily broken down without decay and no by-products hence it is alactacid.

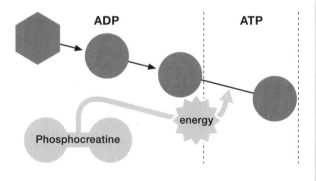

Energy restored in this way can sustain exercise for between 8–10 seconds before all PC stores are used. Source 2 is then used.

2 Lactic acid system or glycolysis

As exercise continues beyond 10 seconds another method of regenerating ADP to ATP must be found once all available PC is used up.

The second method involves converting energy from food we consume into useable energy in the body. We do this by the partial breakdown of glucose which occurs if there is insufficient O_2 to completely breakdown glucose. Glucose is stored in the muscles and liver as **glycogen** and its breakdown is called **glycolysis**.

Glycogen ($C_6H_{12}O_6$)is a complex compound that stores lots of energy in its links, when the enzyme **phosphorylase** is present it breaks down to glucose. Glucose then further breaks down when **phospho-fructokinase** (be careful how you say this!) is present and active. This occurs when concentration of phosphocreatine are low and calcium (used to stimulate Huxleys sliding filament) are high. The glucose breaks down to pyruvic acid. This further breaks down to lactic acid when O_2 is absent.

This system is not as instantaneous as the PC system as more reactions must take place, but it is still relatively fast hence high energy events, e.g. 400 m run, can be sustained.

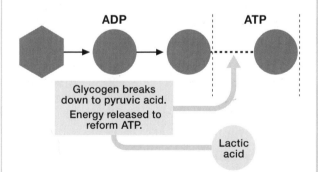

Energy restored in this way can sustain exercise for between 30 seconds to 1.00 minute depending upon the fitness level of the performer. After this time energy must be produced in a different way.

The recovery process (2)

> *The process by which the body returns to pre-exercise state.*

3 The aerobic system

Limited amounts of O_2 are stored in the muscles of the body in association with myoglobin. This is insufficient however to help produce energy efficiently with food fuels in the body hence the reliance on the anaerobic systems at the start of exercise. As exercise continues and heart rate and ventilation increase so does the amount of oxygen in the working muscles. This allows the more efficient breakdown of glucose via aerobic respiration. This leads to complete breakdown of glucose releasing vast quantities of energy for ADP resynthesis, albeit very slowly.

This occurs through 3 stages:

1 Aerobic glycolysis

Glucose is broken down to pyruvic acid and as there is sufficient O_2 available no lactic acid is produced and enough energy is released to resynthesise two molecules of ATP.

2 Krebs cycle/TCA/citric acid cycle

Pyruvic acid enters the mitochondria to be broken down to acetyl where it combines with coenzyme A (CoA) to form (acetyl–CoA).

A cyclical set of reactions takes place which leads to the release of large amounts of energy to resynthesise two molecules of ATP.

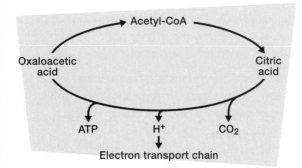

3 Electron transport chain

Hydrogen released in stage two enters the inner membranes of the mitochondria. Electrons removed from hydrogen are combined with O_2 to form water, along the way energy is released to reform 34 molecules of ATP.

The aerobic system is the most efficient method of producing energy in terms of easily disposable waste products – but it takes time due to the reactions required. ATP is therefore regenerated more slowly hence the athlete performs at a lower energy level, e.g. long distance events slower than sprints.

What changes occur in the body during exercise?

1 ATP levels decrease

2 Phosphocreatine levels decrease

3 Glycogen levels decrease

4 Triglyceride levels decrease

5 Oxygen/myoglobin levels decrease

6 Carbon dioxide levels increase

7 Lactic acid levels increase.

How does the body reverse these changes?

The body must 'work' to reverse these changes and there is a cost in energy to do this. The body does not immediately return to resting levels of heart rate or breathing rate. This increased aerobic respiration rate is used to repay the **oxygen debt**. This is the amount of oxygen consumed above resting levels for the same time period following exercise.

What is oxygen deficit?

Oxygen deficit is the amount of energy, therefore oxygen consumption, required to reform all of the phosphocreatine and glycogen used during the early stages of exercise when there was insufficient oxygen available.

Oxygen debt

Oxygen debt has two components.

Alactacid component

This is repaid very rapidly and is used to resynthesise ATP and phosphocreatine which are depleted during exercise. Full replenishment after exercise may take 2–3 minutes and uses typically up to 4 litres of oxygen depending upon the intensity of exercise.

Games players can use this information to take rests when possible to allow replenishment of high energy stores, e.g. time outs in basketball; penalties, lineouts, scrums in rugby.

Time may not be available for full recovery but some return to resting levels of ATP and PC will occur. This will prevent further reliance on the lactic acid system.

Lactacid component

Lactic acid accumulates in the muscle and blood during intense activity. It is removed in four ways and can take up to four hours after exercise has ceased to be completely removed.

60% of lactic acid is converted back to pyruvic acid and then used as a source of energy in the Krebs cycle. To convert this costs energy hence increased respiration above resting values after exercise has finished. Gentle exercise or warm-down is of benefit in this process as this maintains higher respiration rate but also flushes lactic acid out of fast twitch fibres, the remaining 40% is converted to protein or muscle glycogen or it is sweated or excreted from the body.

50% of all the lactic acid is removed in the first 1/2 hour after exercise and uses typically 5–8 litres of oxygen.

Myoglobin and oxygen stores

Myoglobin at rest stores oxygen within the muscles cells (it is similar to haemaglobin in the blood). During exercise it shuttles oxygen from the capillaries to the mitochondria. After intense exercise the myoglobin–oxygen stores are very depleted.

Oxygen stored in the muscle is useful because it helps to 'spare' phosphocreatine and glycogen at the beginning of exercise because the body can supply some of its needs aerobically. This store is quickly depleted. It is restored only when there is a surplus of oxygen in the system following exercise.

Elevated respiration rates following exercise means spare oxygen is available to replenish stored stock.

Glycogen stores

Only very small amounts of glycogen are stored in the body and these can become depleted very quickly when it is used for aerobic and anaerobic work. After two hours of intensive exercise, stores of glycogen will be running low.

(This is most often seen when fun runners hit 'the wall' in the marathon and they begin to lose control of their coordination.)

Glycogen is important as a source of high energy fuel, it is vital that it is spared during exercise to ensure it is there when the athlete needs it. Stores can be replaced by eating a high carbohydrate meal following exercise.

> Athletes must learn to pace themselves during exercise to avoid crossing the 'anaerobic threshold'
> Athletes must learn to take rests during activity to allow phosphogen and myoglobin stores to recover (this spares glycogen use)
> Replenish stores of glycogen during exercise by taking small but regular amounts of glucose drinks.

Aerobic training allows the preferential use of fats as an energy source during sub-maximal exercise thus sparing glycogen.

The concept of an energy continuum

> *Applying energy systems to various activities.*

The three energy systems do not work independently of each other, but in unison and in response to the changing demands of the environment the body is working in.

Most sporting activities require a mix of energy – thus all three systems contribute as athletes cross the threshold (the point at which it is inefficient to produce energy via that system) of the three systems.

This is why fartlek training is so effective for games players.

We can represent the contributions made by energy systems in broad terms on a continuum.

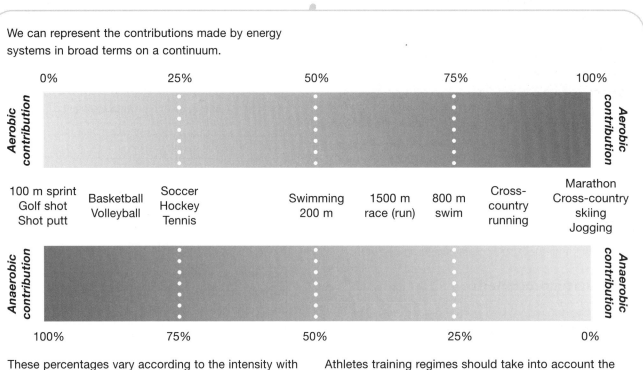

	0%	25%	50%	75%	100%	
Aerobic contribution						*Aerobic contribution*

| 100 m sprint Golf shot Shot putt | Basketball Volleyball | Soccer Hockey Tennis | Swimming 200 m | 1500 m race (run) | 800 m swim | Cross-country running | Marathon Cross-country skiing Jogging |

| *Anaerobic contribution* | 100% | 75% | 50% | 25% | 0% | *Anaerobic contribution* |

These percentages vary according to the intensity with which each activity is performed, e.g. a competitive soccer match will use more anaerobic energy than a friendly kick about in the park amongst friends.

Athletes training regimes should take into account the requirements for energy in order to make training as specific as possible.

$\dot{V}O_2$ max

The amount of energy used during exercise is directly related to the amount of oxygen consumed.

The breakdown of glycogen and fat requires the presence of oxygen.

If we measure the amount of oxygen consumed (by comparing expired oxygen content with atmospheric air oxygen content) we can estimate the amount of energy used.

At rest we consume 0.2–0.3 litres of oxygen per minute.

VO_2 – v = volume per minute, O_2 = oxygen

During **maximal** exercise this may rise to 3–6 litres of oxygen per minute ($\dot{V}O_2$ max).

An athlete's $\dot{V}O_2$ max is determined by the efficiency of their cardiac system, respiratory system, and other physiological characteristics, e.g. muscle fibre types.

$\dot{V}O_2$ max may be improved by training – increased capillarisation, increase in red blood cells, increased cardiac output, increased myoglobin content, increase in size and number of mitochondria – by up to 20%.

Physical fitness

> *Parts of fitness.*

Health components

Aerobic capacity

This is the ability of a performer to take in and use oxygen. This depends upon:

1 Respiration (external)
2 Oxygen transportation from lungs to muscles
3 Cell respiration.

> This is often referred to as **maximal oxygen consumption** (or '$\dot{V}O_2$ max') – sub-maximal activity benefits aerobic capacity (e.g. jogging, cycling, swimming).

Strength

This is the amount of force a performer can exert through their muscles. Maximum strength is one single contraction. Dynamic strength or power is the ability to overcome resistance very quickly and is used in nearly all sports.

Muscular endurance is the ability to contract the muscles again and again without growing tired. This is a vital aspect of fitness for all sports people – as a match progresses fatigue sets in; the team that resists fatiguing best often wins.

Flexibility

This is the ability to move body parts around a joint.

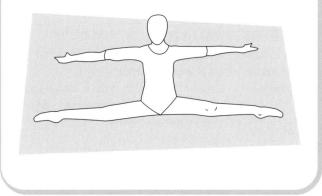

Body composition

This refers to the relative percentage of overall weight that various components of the body make up (e.g. bones, blood, muscle, organs [lean body mass] and fat).

Principles of training

> *Improving the training effect.*

Overload

The human body is designed to adapt to new demands made on it. So if we put the body under more strain, it will respond by changing to meet the new demands.

Overload is achieved by:

F > Increasing the number of times you train or the frequency. **Frequency**

I > Increasing the amount of work you do in a session, the intensity. **Intensity**

T > Increasing the length of time that you train. **Time**

Specificity

> Fitness is made up of lots of different components. The type of fitness required by different sports is quite different. Therefore your training should reflect the demands of your sport.

> Your training should mimic the type of movements required by that sport.

> Everyone is different, therefore your training should be specific to you – measure the components shown to identify weak areas upon which you can make improvements.

> Most sports use very specific energy systems at specific times. Try to reflect these differences in your training.

Reversibility

Fitness cannot be banked to be used in the future. Any changes due to training will reverse once training is stopped.

Variance

Try to spice up your training by doing different things, using different methods to prevent boredom.

Beware: repetitive strain injuries!

Skill components

Speed – the ability to move your body quickly.

Reaction time – the time taken to respond to a stimulus.

Agility – the ability to change direction of speed efficiently.

Balance – achieved when the centre of mass of a performer is over an area of support.

Coordination – the ability to move in a smooth and efficient manner to achieve a particular task. This involves ensuring motor programmes run in the correct order.

All of these aspects can be evaluated and measured, which allows the athlete to identify a starting point for training and to monitor improvements in each aspect.

Training programmes

> *How to improve health components of fitness.*

These must be specific to the needs of your activity and follow the principle of training. They will affect the health-related and skill-related components of your fitness.

Strength training

Strength is improved by increasing the level of resistance that a muscle group must overcome (overload). Athletes must decide very carefully what type of strength they wish to improve (see descriptions on physical fitness, page 59) and which specific muscles to work on, and the type of contraction required by their sport.

Absolute strength will be improved by working with greater resistances (more weight) and fewer repetitions per set. Muscular endurance will be improved by working with lower resistances (less weight) but more repetitions per set.

Repetition is a full contraction of a muscular group during an exercise (e.g. biceps curl and a return to its original position).

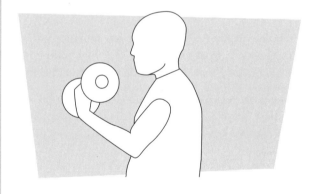

A set is a number of repetitions of a given exercise (this will depend on the type of strength being improved).

Methods to improve strength

Weight training – the use of free weights on dumbbells and bars which can allow the athlete to mimic closely some of the actions involved in his/her sport or the use of specially designed (safer) machines to work on.

Circuit training – often using the performer's body weight on a number of exercises to improve strength, particularly good for young children (e.g. press ups, sit ups, dips, running).

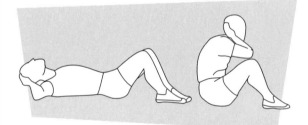

Plyometrics – muscles working eccentrically, then immediately concentrically – improve muscle strength dramatically (e.g. triple jumping, running down hill).

Flexibility – a performer's flexibility is limited by the structures in the joints. Bony structures cannot change, nor can the movements allowed by certain joint types. However, soft tissues – such as ligaments, tendons and muscles – can be stretched.

Improvements in flexibility can be rapid and occur to their greatest extent when the body is already warm. Too much mobility in some joints, especially in contact sports, can lead to injury. Training of this component must be very specific.

Aerobic training

> *Improving the oxygen transport system.*

Aerobic training

These are designed to increase $\dot{V}O_2$ max and will involve sub-maximal activity. Remember, working above the 'anaerobic threshold' will work only the lactacid system. However, you must still overload your system.

Researchers suggest that continuous exercise for at least 20 minutes above a critical level is necessary. You should begin gently but increase the frequency, intensity or duration of the session if you are able to perform the training at a lower heart rate than previously.

Methods to improve $\dot{V}O_2$ max
> Choose a rhythmic activity (e.g. swimming, jogging, cycling, aerobics) that uses large muscles.
> Work in your aerobic training zone. This means at least 60% of your maximum heart rate, unless you are very fit. As you get fitter, you can move up to 75%.
> For best results: at least 15–20 minutes at least 3 times a week.

> You can use this sort of training for things like running, cycling and skiing.
> The principle is that during a continuous run, periods of more intense work are used to stress the systems, but recovery is allowed during the slower periods. This is useful as it follows the principle of variance and is good for athletes who need to 'change pace' as part of their game.

Fartlek or 'speed play'

> This is based on changes of speed. For instance, 5 minutes of gentle jogging; then 5 minutes of fast walk; then 50 m sprints every 200 m; then uphill jog with 10 fast strides every minute; and so on...

Interval training

This is training where 'work' periods are interspersed with 'rest' periods to allow recovery. It is very good for maintaining quality training, particularly in elite athletes.

Methods to improve flexibility

Active stretching

The performer moves their own body into a position just beyond the normal range and holds that position for 10 seconds. This is known as **active stretching**.

Passive stretching

Passive stretching involves the body being moved by a partner to a position beyond the normal range of movement and then being held for 10 seconds.

Ballistic stretching

This involves swinging/bouncing movements to take the body beyond its normal range of movement. Only athletes with a good level of flexibility should use this method.

Proprioceptive Neuro-muscular Facilitation (PNF)

The performer stretches to a point just beyond the normal range of movement. The athlete contracts the muscle, then relaxes, and then takes the stretch a little further.

Short-term effects of exercise

> *What happens during exercise.*

The human body is constantly battling with changing circumstances to maintain a stable, efficient internal condition. The responses shown below are the ways in which the body tries to maintain **homeostasis** (controlled environment within cells).

Heart

Exercise changes the chemical balance of the body:
> lactic acid increases
> CO_2 + O_2 levels change
> and temperature increases.

This produces stimuli for the cardiac control centre to respond to.

Nerves: the sympathetic nerve controlling the sino-atrial node (pacemaker) is stimulated to increase heart rate.

Chemical: adrenaline is released in the blood increasing heart rate even before exercise.

Cardiac output increases because the heart rate increases; venous return increases which in turn increases the amount of blood entering the heart. More blood in the heart and stronger more frequent contractions leads to increased cardiac output (Q).

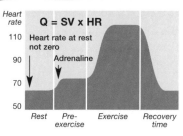

Heart rate

Q = SV x HR

110 Heart rate at rest not zero

90 Adrenaline

70

50

Rest   Pre-exercise   Exercise   Recovery time

Lungs

Changes to the relative proportions of CO_2 and O_2 are detected in the respiratory centre, which responds by increasing minute ventilation.

Minute ventilation is a function of the number of breaths and the tidal volume. Tidal volume increases by drawing upon the spare lung capacity, known as inspiratory reserve volume and expiratory reserve volume.

The respiratory muscles, intercostals, diaphragm and scaleni become more active, especially on expiration. This increases the volume of the thoracic cavity and decreases it with greater force.

Blood

> Blood changes its constitution during exercise. This carries the messages that are detected by receptors to initiate changes in HR and ventilation.
> Blood becomes thicker during intense activity as plasma volume decreases due to sweating.
> Glucose levels begin to drop.
> Blood acidity increases due to lactic acid. This may, if not controlled, lead to a detrimental effect on muscle activity.
> Oxygen concentrations drop dramatically, thus increasing diffusion at the lungs.
> Blood pressure increases as Q increases.
> Blood flow speeds up.
> More blood is directed to the muscles and away from other areas. Vasodilation in arteries to muscles and in muscle capillaries aids blood flow here.
> Vasoconstriction around non-essential areas decreases blood flow in these areas.

Muscles

Increases in the intensity and frequency of contractions lead to a greater use of energy, thus increasing cell respiration. These changes stimulate the rest of the body to adapt.

The body's fuel energy stores are gradually depleted:
> phospho-creatine
> glycogen
> triglycerides (free fatty acids).

The myoglobin in the muscles gives up its oxygen stores for cell respiration. Thus O_2 is diffused more quickly as the partial pressure difference between cell and capillary is greater.

Carbon dioxide and lactic acid levels increase in the muscles and need to be removed by the blood.

The energy conversion in the muscle is notoriously inefficient. It is only between 14–25% efficient, with most energy being released as heat, thus increasing body temperature.

But what about the longer-term effects....?

Long-term effects of exercise

> *Training causes long-term adaptations in body systems to cope with the new demands made.*

Aerobic changes

An improvement in an athlete's $\dot{V}O_2$ max occurs during correct aerobic exercise routines. Most of the time the athlete's muscles depend on aerobic respiration.

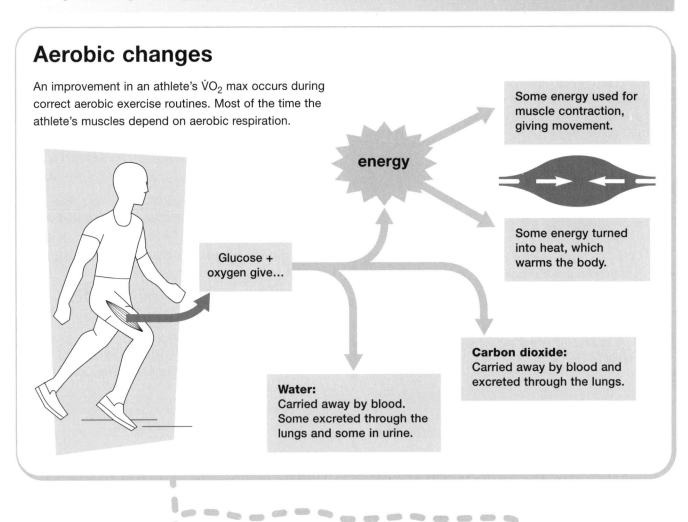

energy

Some energy used for muscle contraction, giving movement.

Glucose + oxygen give...

Some energy turned into heat, which warms the body.

Water:
Carried away by blood. Some excreted through the lungs and some in urine.

Carbon dioxide:
Carried away by blood and excreted through the lungs.

1 Heart

> The muscles of the heart wall (myocardium) grow in size and strength after regular exercise. This allows the heart to contract with more force, therefore ejecting more blood per heart beat.

> Increased heart size means increased stroke volume. Therefore at rest the athlete's heart has to pump less times to move the same amount of blood as an untrained heart. This results in lower resting heart rate (bradycardia).

> At maximum levels of effort, stroke volume is increased and heart rate is high. Thus more O_2 is delivered to the working muscles increasing efficiency and increasing $\dot{V}O_2$ max.

2 Lungs

> Maximum minute volume is increased.

> The respiratory muscles are stronger and more efficient, making respiration easier.

> Lung capacity improves as training increases. Capillarisation around the alveoli allows greater areas of lung to be utilized.

Anaerobic changes

During all-out effort, such as sprinting, the muscles need a lot of energy fast. Because oxygen cannot reach the muscles fast enough, **anaerobic respiration** takes over. Less energy is produced from the same amount of glucose, but it is produced much faster.

> Anaerobic training allows athletes to work harder and for longer at higher intensities.

> Muscles, particularly fibre types 2a and 2b, grow in size and therefore strength.

> Stores of ATP (see page 54) are increased.

> Phosphocreatine and glycogen are produced.

> The enzyme phosphorylase increases in concentration allowing more efficient resynthesis of ADP to ATP.

> There is an increased tolerance of lactic acid in the muscles and the recovery system for its removal also more efficient.

Some energy used for muscle contraction, giving movement.

energy

Very fast

Some energy turned into heat, which warms the body.

Glucose gives...

Oxygen can't reach muscle fast enough

Lactic acid:
After a minute or so, lactic acid makes muscles tired and painful. All-out effort must stop or you'll collapse.

3 Blood

> Volume of blood increases, due mostly to increased plasma levels. More red blood cells are also created, allowing greater oxygen-carrying capacity.

> Acidity of the blood decreases at low level exercise as their aerobic system is more efficient.

> At maximal levels of exercise, blood acidity is higher in athletes as they have a greater tolerance of its effects.

> Arterial walls become more elastic with endurance training, allowing tolerance of changes in blood pressure. There is greater capillarisation in the lungs and muscles allowing greater diffusion of O_2.

4 Muscles

> Muscles grow larger and stronger through exercise.

> Myoglobin concentration increases.

> Mitochondria become more numerous.

> Enzymes work much more efficiently allowing greater cell respiration.

> Muscles store larger amounts of glycogen and triglycerides.

Linear motion – distance, velocity and acceleration

> Vectors or scalars? When they are the same and when they are different.

We will start this topic by looking at 'linear motion'. What is 'linear motion'? A simple definition might be 'movement forward or backward in a generally straight line'.

Make a list in a notebook of all the sports you can think of which involve a 'linear motion'. How can we measure this motion? To start with we need to consider the following:

> **distance** – the path taken by an object moving from one point to another

> **displacement** – the shortest straight line between the starting and finishing point ('as the crow flies')

> **speed** – rate of change of position; the distance travelled by the body per unit time

> **velocity** – rate of change of position with reference to direction

> **acceleration** – rate of change in velocity.

Key points:

1 **Vector quantities** are those with both magnitude and direction. They include: displacement, velocity, acceleration and force.

2 **Scalar quantities** are those with just magnitude. They include: distance, speed and mass (amount of matter).

Distance and Displacement

It is possible to have an equal value for these measures, as is the case when considering a 100 m sprint. Here the path taken by the runner measures 100 metres. The distance from the starting point to the finish point is also 100 metres.

This is not the case in a 100 m swim (2 x 50 m lengths). Here, the path taken by the swimmer is 100 metres, whilst the distance from the starting point to the finish point is 0! (They start and end at the same end of the pool.)

Speed and Velocity

The difference between distance and displacement has an effect on calculations. If the swimmer covers 100 m in 60 seconds then the average speed will be:

$$\frac{\text{Distance}}{\text{Time}} = \frac{100}{60} = 1.67 \text{ ms}^{-1}$$

But the average velocity will be:

$$\frac{\text{Displacement}}{\text{Time}} = \frac{0}{60} = 0 \text{ ms}^{-1}$$

Averages

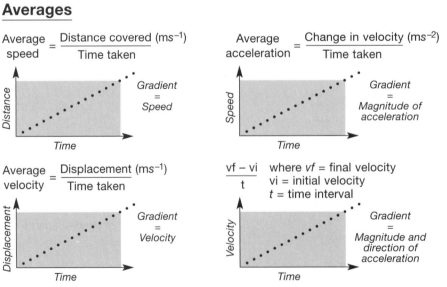

$$\text{Average speed} = \frac{\text{Distance covered (ms}^{-1})}{\text{Time taken}}$$

Gradient = Speed (Distance vs Time)

$$\text{Average velocity} = \frac{\text{Displacement (ms}^{-1})}{\text{Time taken}}$$

Gradient = Velocity (Displacement vs Time)

$$\text{Average acceleration} = \frac{\text{Change in velocity (ms}^{-2})}{\text{Time taken}}$$

Gradient = Magnitude of acceleration (Speed vs Time)

$$\frac{vf - vi}{t}$$ where *vf* = final velocity
vi = initial velocity
t = time interval

Gradient = Magnitude and direction of acceleration (Velocity vs Time)

Note: Displacement, velocity and acceleration are all *vector* quantities and can therefore be used together in equations. Speed and distance are *scalar* quantities and also appear together in equations. **Do NOT mix vector (those with magnitude and direction) and scalar quantities (those with only magnitude) in equations!**

Vectors

Vectors are quantities such as displacement, velocity, acceleration and force (which includes weight!) which have both *magnitude* and *direction*. We can represent a vector by a line with an arrow on the end. The length of the line represents the magnitude of the vector and the arrow indicates the direction.

Examples

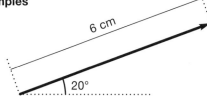

1 Using a scale of 1 cm = 1 ms⁻¹, this line represents a velocity of 6 ms⁻¹ at an angle of 20° to the horizontal.

This principle may be used for all vectors.

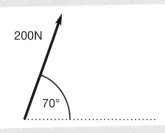

2 Here we have a force of 200 N acting at 70° to the horizontal.

Note: Because we can represent vectors as a combination of length and angle, we can use a range of trigonometric techniques to calculate answers to problems.

Resultant vectors

When two or more vectors are combined, their overall effect is described as being their **resultant vector**. Consider the two velocities (a) and (b) below. We can combine them by making the arrows 'follow on'. The resultant is the overall effect of the two arrows 'following on' (c).

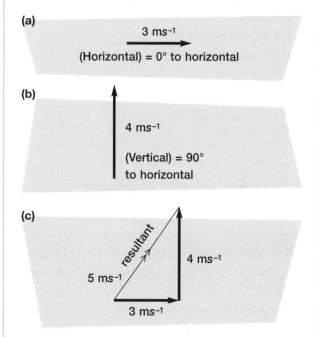

The resultant vector can be measured directly with a ruler for magnitude and a protractor for direction, if velocities are drawn to scale. This is known as the construction technique. Alternatively, the results may be calculated using Pythagoras or other trigonometric rules.

(Notice how the example given is almost instantly observed as being a '3, 4, 5 triangle'!)

Component vectors

A similar technique may be used to 'dismantle' a vector into two components. This is called **resolving** into horizontal and vertical components. It involves producing horizontal and vertical 'follow on' vectors from a single vector (the reverse of resultant vectors).

Example

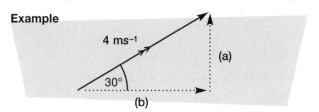

Here the velocity of 4 ms⁻¹ has been resolved into horizontal and vertical vectors that 'follow on'. The magnitude of these vectors can be measured directly with a ruler, if drawn to scale (construction technique), but are calculated using the following rule:

> Vector opposite angle (a) = hypotenuse sine angle = 4 sin 30° = 2
>
> Vector adjacent angle (b) = hypotenuse cosine angle = 4 cos 30° = 3.46 ms⁻¹

Projectile motion

> *The interplay between horizontal and vertical components during the flight of a projectile.*

Definition

A body that is released into the air.

Examples

Throwing, striking, projecting of the body itself.

The projectile's pre-determined path of flight (parabola) is influenced by:

1 the force applied, establishing its velocity at release

2 the angle of release

3 the relative height of release.

1 Speed or velocity of release

> The greater the speed of release, the greater the range.

> The speed of release has a greater influence on the range of a projectile than the angle or relative height.

> The greater the initial vertical velocity, the greater the flight time and the greater the height reached.

> The greater the initial horizontal velocity, the greater the horizontal distance.

> The lower the angle of release, the greater the release velocity must be if the projectile is to travel the required distance.

A body projected at 30 ms^{-1} at an angle θ to the horizontal.

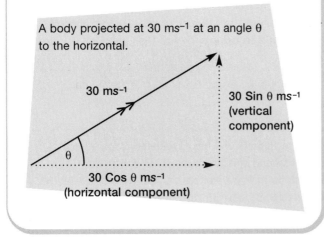

30 ms^{-1}

30 Sin θ ms^{-1} (vertical component)

θ

30 Cos θ ms^{-1} (horizontal component)

2 Angle of release

> The optimum angle at which you need to project a body in order to obtain the maximum horizontal range is **45°**. This only applies where the **release** and **landing** occur at the **same** level, and where there is no spin and no air assistance.

> In most sporting situations, the angle is almost always less than 45° => in range 35°–45°.

> If the angle of release is too high, the horizontal component of velocity is reduced, thus reducing the horizontal distance.

> If the angle of release is too low, the vertical component of velocity is reduced, thus reducing the time of flight which, in turn, reduces the horizontal distance (less **time** for horizontal component of velocity to act).

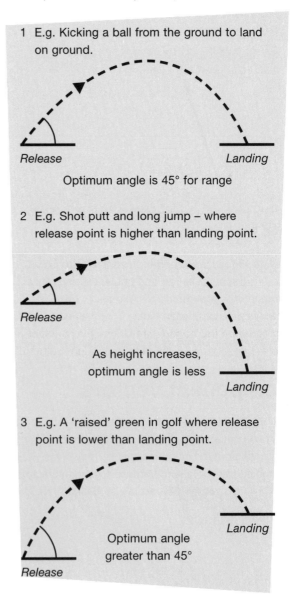

1 E.g. Kicking a ball from the ground to land on ground.

Release

Landing

Optimum angle is 45° for range

2 E.g. Shot putt and long jump – where release point is higher than landing point.

Release

As height increases, optimum angle is less

Landing

3 E.g. A 'raised' green in golf where release point is lower than landing point.

Landing

Optimum angle greater than 45°

Release

3 Relative height of release

> For a given speed and angle of release, as the relative height increases, the horizontal range increases.

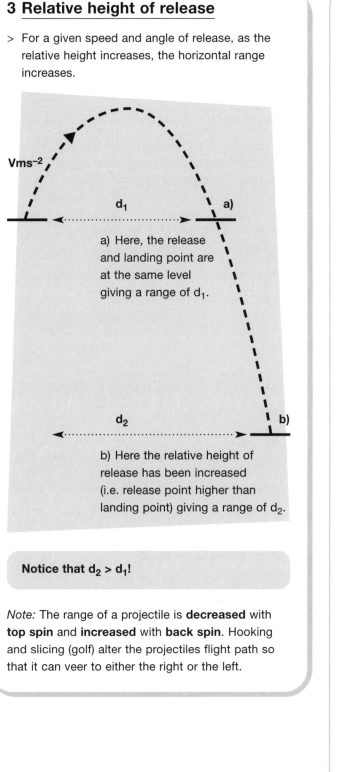

Vms⁻²

d₁

a)

a) Here, the release and landing point are at the same level giving a range of d₁.

d₂

b)

b) Here the relative height of release has been increased (i.e. release point higher than landing point) giving a range of d₂.

Notice that d₂ > d₁!

Note: The range of a projectile is **decreased** with **top spin** and **increased** with **back spin**. Hooking and slicing (golf) alter the projectiles flight path so that it can veer to either the right or the left.

The changes in the vertical and horizontal components

E.g. Shot putt

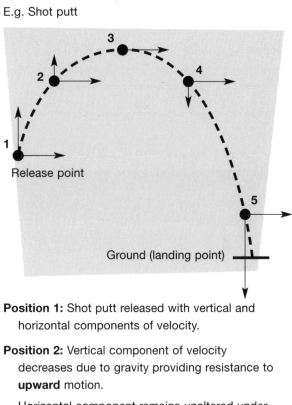

3

2

4

1

Release point

5

Ground (landing point)

Position 1: Shot putt released with vertical and horizontal components of velocity.

Position 2: Vertical component of velocity decreases due to gravity providing resistance to **upward** motion.

Horizontal component remains unaltered under the assumption that air resistance is negligible (air resistance is the only force that **could** act horizontally to slow the shot down!).

Position 3: Shot at top of flight path therefore **no** vertical component (gravity has acted to reduce this to zero).

Horizontal component remains unaltered (air resistance negligible).

Position 4: Vertical component equal in magnitude but opposite in direction to position 2 as these points are level on a parabolic path.

Horizontal component remains constant (air resistance negligible).

Position 5: Vertical component acts downward and is at its greatest in terms of magnitude due to gravity accelerating the shot. It is greater than in position 1 as gravity has acted for longer (i.e. it is a point just before landing and therefore lower than the release point).

Horizontal component remains constant (air resistance negligible).

Linear motion – forces, Newton's Laws

> *Forces acting **on a body** and forces applied **by a body**.*

A force is a push or a pull that acts on an object in order to change its state of motion.

Forces may be **internal** (those generated by ourselves through muscular contraction) and **external** (those from outside our body such as gravity, friction, air resistance and those caused by reactions with the ground or some other external body).

Forces are *vector* quantities and therefore have magnitude and direction. They can be represented by a line of action and a point of application.

When considering forces, it is necessary to distinguish between those forces acting on the body and those applied by the body *separately*. This normally involves the consideration of external forces. This will help when analysing the interaction of two or more bodies.

Forces are measured in Newtons!

Example

In order to understand the force acting in the use of the scrummage machine we need to consider:

(a) the forces exerted **by** the rugby player(s) and forces acting on the machine

(b) the forces acting **on** the rugby player and forces exerted by the machine.

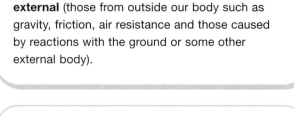

(a) Forces acting on the machine

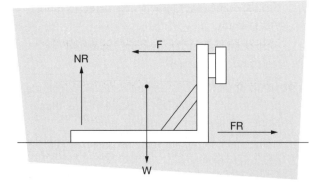

NR = Normal Reaction force from contact with ground

W = Weight of scrummage machine (acting through centre of gravity of machine)

F = Action force applied by player

FR = Friction force from ground contact opposing sliding motion of scrummage machine

(b) Forces acting on the player

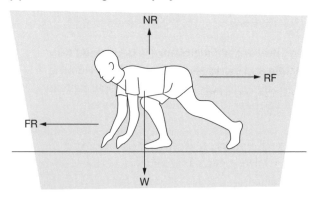

NR = Net normal reaction force from contacts with ground

W = Weight of rugby player

RF = Reaction force from scrummage machine

FR = Friction force from ground contact opposing sliding motion of feet and hands

Newton's First Law

> This is the law of inertia which states that:

'Every object will remain in a state of rest or uniform motion unless acted upon by an external force.'

> Also known as 'Galileo's law'.

> 'Inertia' is an object's reluctance to move. So this law is often linked to inertia. Inertia is proportional to mass and therefore more force is required to move a heavy object than a light one.

> In the sprint start, the athlete will not move unless a 'net' external force acts upon him/her. Thus a force needs to be applied to move the athlete from (a) to (b) to (c).

(a) 'On your marks'

(b) 'Get set'

(c) 'GO!!'

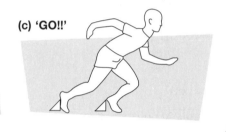

Newton's Second Law

> This law states that:

'The rate of change of momentum or acceleration of an object is proportional to the force applied and acts in the direction of the force.'

> 'Momentum' is defined as the amount of motion.

Momentum = Mass x Velocity

This may be written as:

$$F = \frac{Mvf - Mvi}{t}$$

where F = Force, Mvf = Final momentum, Mvi = Initial momentum, t = time

Rewriting gives:

$$F = \frac{M(vf - vi)}{t}$$

But!

$$\frac{vf - vi}{t} = acceleration$$

so F (force) = mass x acceleration

> In the sprint start, the athlete will accelerate more with a great net force acting.

Newton's Third Law

> This law states that:

'When one object exerts a force on another, there is a force equal in magnitude but opposite in direction exerted by the second object on the first.'

OR

Action and reaction are equal and opposite.

> This means that when the sprinter exerts a downward and backwards force against the blocks – in (c), the blocks exert an upward and forward reaction force on the sprinter.

> *But* if the action and reaction forces are equal and opposite, why does the sprinter move?

The answer lies with the significant differences between the mass of the sprinter and the mass of the Earth. As the blocks are *fixed* to the Earth, they become part of the Earth's mass. Therefore, the force applied by the runner is not enough to displace such a large mass. The reaction force from the blocks is enough, however, to displace the relatively small mass of the sprinter!

Newton's Laws are the basic laws of mechanics that describe the way in which bodies move in response to forces acting on them.

Linear motion – impulse

> *The relationship between impulse, force and acceleration.*

Impulse is the change in linear motion caused by a force. So a given impulse can be associated with a weak force over a long time, or with a strong force acting over a short time. The latter is termed an **impulsive force**.

Forces in a vertical jump

Consider the forces acting in a vertical jump.

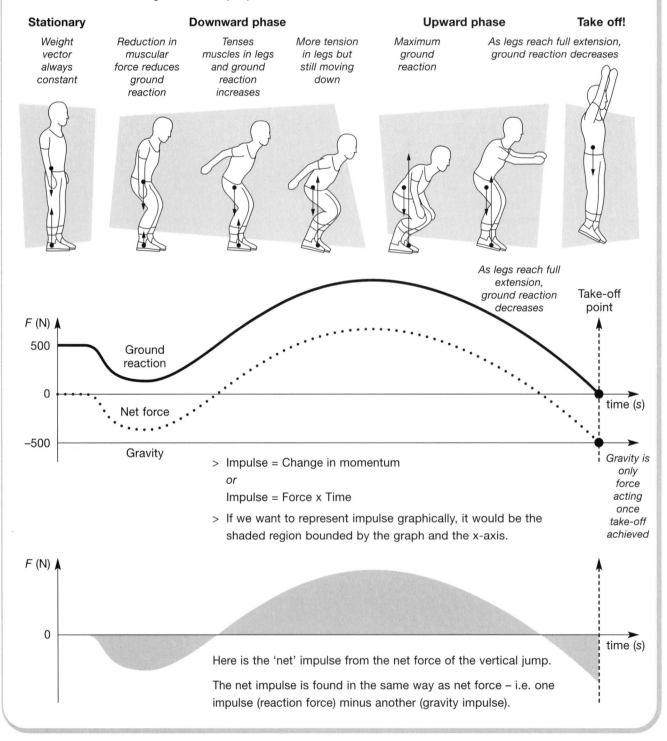

Stationary

Weight vector always constant

Downward phase

Reduction in muscular force reduces ground reaction

Tenses muscles in legs and ground reaction increases

More tension in legs but still moving down

Upward phase

Maximum ground reaction

As legs reach full extension, ground reaction decreases

Take off!

As legs reach full extension, ground reaction decreases

Take-off point

F (N)

500

Ground reaction

0

Net force

time (s)

−500

Gravity

Gravity is only force acting once take-off achieved

> Impulse = Change in momentum

or

Impulse = Force x Time

> If we want to represent impulse graphically, it would be the shaded region bounded by the graph and the x-axis.

F (N)

0

time (s)

Here is the 'net' impulse from the net force of the vertical jump.

The net impulse is found in the same way as net force – i.e. one impulse (reaction force) minus another (gravity impulse).

Forces in a sprint start

Now consider a sprint start (100 metres).

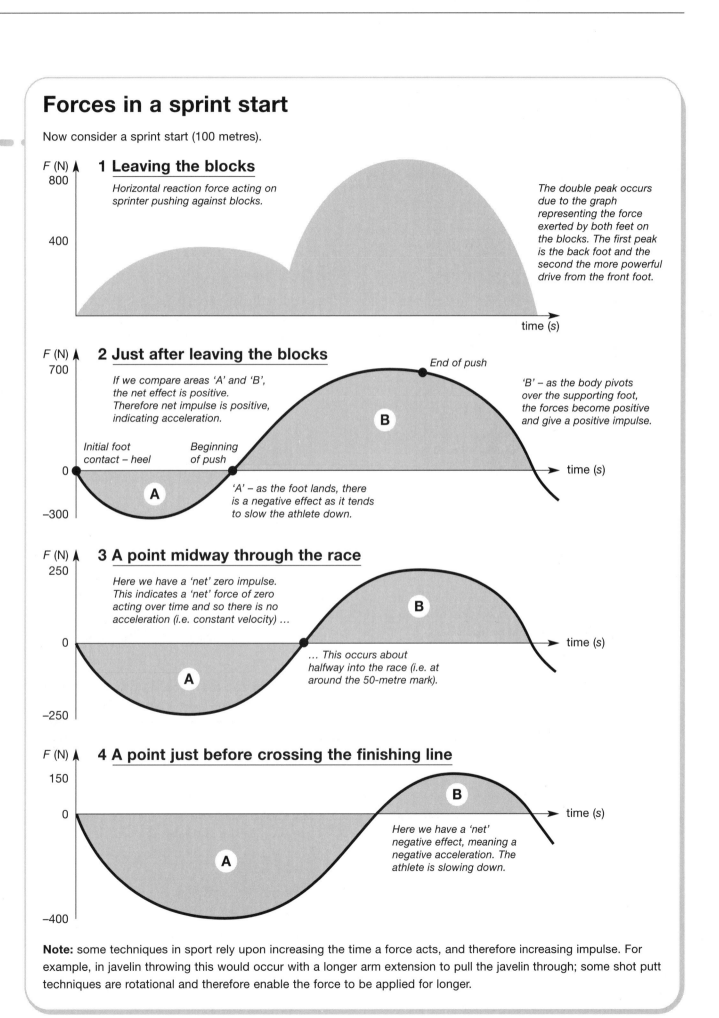

1 Leaving the blocks

F (N)

Horizontal reaction force acting on sprinter pushing against blocks.

The double peak occurs due to the graph representing the force exerted by both feet on the blocks. The first peak is the back foot and the second the more powerful drive from the front foot.

time (s)

2 Just after leaving the blocks

F (N)

If we compare areas 'A' and 'B', the net effect is positive. Therefore net impulse is positive, indicating acceleration.

End of push

'B' – as the body pivots over the supporting foot, the forces become positive and give a positive impulse.

Initial foot contact – heel

Beginning of push

B

A

'A' – as the foot lands, there is a negative effect as it tends to slow the athlete down.

time (s)

3 A point midway through the race

F (N)

Here we have a 'net' zero impulse. This indicates a 'net' force of zero acting over time and so there is no acceleration (i.e. constant velocity) ...

B

A

... This occurs about halfway into the race (i.e. at around the 50-metre mark).

time (s)

4 A point just before crossing the finishing line

F (N)

B

A

Here we have a 'net' negative effect, meaning a negative acceleration. The athlete is slowing down.

time (s)

Note: some techniques in sport rely upon increasing the time a force acts, and therefore increasing impulse. For example, in javelin throwing this would occur with a longer arm extension to pull the javelin through; some shot putt techniques are rotational and therefore enable the force to be applied for longer.

Linear motion – pressure and friction

> *The interplay of forces and surfaces.*

> > **Pressure** is the force per unit area applied to a surface.

> > **Friction** is the force acting between two surfaces parallel to the surfaces in contact.

Pressure

> When a person stands on the floor in an upright position, the supporting area of his/her feet will experience a ground reaction force (RF). This will be equal and opposite to the weight of the person (W).

> This reaction force does not pass through a single point but is distributed over the supporting area of the feet.

> The pressure is calculated by

$$\text{Pressure} = \frac{\text{Force}}{\text{Area}} \quad (\text{N/m}^2 \text{ or } \text{Nm}^{-2})$$

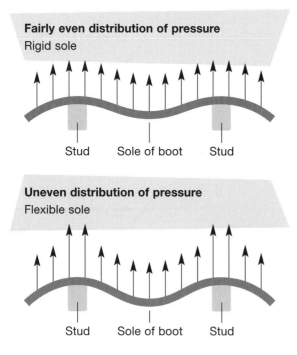

Fairly even distribution of pressure
Rigid sole

Stud   Sole of boot   Stud

Uneven distribution of pressure
Flexible sole

Stud   Sole of boot   Stud

Notice how pressure pays a major part in the choice of footwear.

Friction

This opposes movement or the tendency to move.

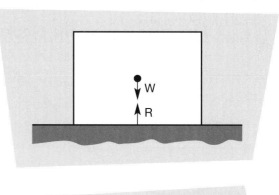

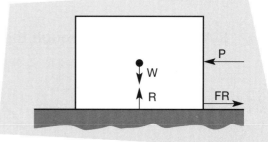

> When stationary, the forces acting on the block are W (Weight) and R (Reaction force from contact with surface).

> If a force P is applied, friction (FR) will begin to come into play to oppose any movement. (Note that until the block begins to move P = FR!)

> Frictional force has a maximum value (i.e. the value just before movement occurs [see note above]). It can be calculated by:

FR = μR

Where: FR = Friction force

μ = Coefficient of friction

R = Reaction force

Note: μ is a measure of the roughness of the two surfaces.

Linear motion – gravity and stability

> *The centre of gravity is crucial in determining stability and balance.*

Gravity

Gravity is a force that acts between two objects in order that they are pulled together. More commonly this relates to the attractive force of the Earth on all objects.

> Newton's Law of Gravitation states:
> **'All particles attract each other with a force proportional to the product of their masses and inversely proportional to the square of the distance between them.'**
>
> Or $F = \dfrac{G M^1 M^2}{d^2}$
>
> where F = force of attraction, G = constant of gravitation, M^1/M^2 are the masses, d = distance

Note: This force of attraction is at its strongest when the distance between the objects is reduced.

Centre of gravity

This is a single point that represents the location of concentration of mass.

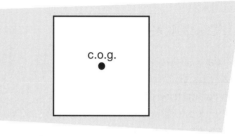

In a block the centre of gravity is 'central' and 'within' the block. But this is not always the case with humans.

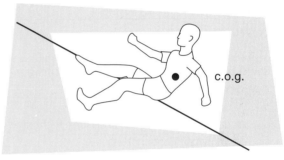

In the 'scissors' high jump technique, the centre of gravity is contained within the body and travels over the bar.

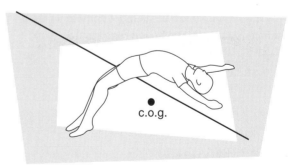

In the Fosbury Flop technique, the centre of gravity is outside the body and travels below the bar.

It is possible to move the position of the centre of gravity by changing body position.

Stability

This is the state of being stable. If your centre of gravity (c.o.g.) shifts, you will become unstable – liable to fall over.

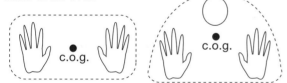

> The headstand has a larger perimeter and therefore area of support. This makes it more stable than the handstand as the centre of gravity would have to move further to be outside the base.

> Consider a rigid bar supported by a hinged base (a). Moving it through an angle of θ would result in the centre of gravity line moving outside the base. The result would be a topple forwards. (b). If we reduce the height of the bar and move it through the same angle, this does not happen.

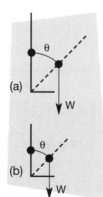

> The weight of an object will also affect stability. Think of Sumo wrestlers!

Linear motion – work, energy and power

> *Measuring efficiency and effectiveness.*

Work

Work is a measure of force acting over a distance. It can be calculated as:

W = F x d

where W = work, F = force and d = distance moved.

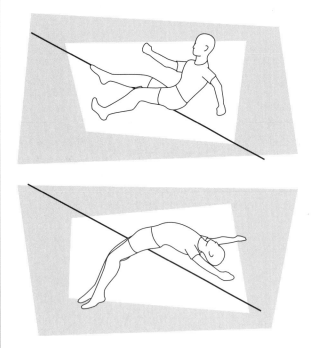

The work done when using the 'scissors' technique is more than in the 'Fosbury Flop'.

This is because in the 'scissors' technique the jumper's centre of gravity has to be moved higher (i.e. above the bar) than in the 'Fosbury Flop'. Therefore more effort and force is required. This is why the Fosbury Flop is the most commonly used technique for high jumping. It requires less work!

Work is measured in Joules (J).

Energy

This is the capacity an object has to do work.

Potential energy

The energy that comes as a result of a specific position relative to reference level. It is found by:

M x g x h

where M = mass, g = acceleration due to gravity (approx. 9.8 ms^{-2}) and h = height.

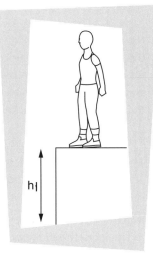

Kinetic energy

The energy that comes as a result of motion. It is found by:

½ x M x v^2

where M = mass and v = velocity

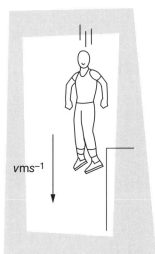

$v$ms^{-1}

Energy is also measured in Joules (J).

Power

This is the rate of doing work.

It is measured in Joules/sec or Watts.

It is calculated by:

$$\text{Power} = \frac{\text{Work}}{\text{Time}}$$

> Work done in a short space of time would be *high power*. Work done (the same amount) in a longer period of time would be *low power*.

Angular motion – distance and displacement

> *Applying linear motion principles to define angular motion.*

The same principles apply to **angular motion** as they do with **linear motion** – except that here they are applied to rotational movement.

Angular distance and displacement

Angular distance is the angle created by a displacement or line at the point of observation.

Angular displacement is the angle through which something has rotated, or the change in the angle.

Let us take a look at the golf swing as an example.

In diagram (a), the golfer has the club at right angles to the ground.

In diagram (b), the club has been taken away through 270°. The angular distance for this movement is 270° rotation but the angular displacement is 90° in an anti-clockwise direction.

> Angular displacement is the smallest angle between the starting and finishing position.

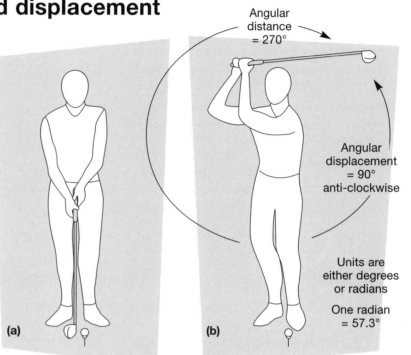

Angular distance = 270°

Angular displacement = 90° anti-clockwise

Units are either degrees or radians

One radian = 57.3°

(a)   **(b)**

Note: when the angle between the starting position and finish position is less than 180°, angular distance and angular displacement are the same.

Angular speed and velocity

Angular speed is the time taken for the angular displacement.

$$\text{Angular speed} = \frac{\text{Angular distance}}{\text{Time}}$$

(°s^{-1}) or (rad.s^{-1})

Angular velocity is the rate of change of angular displacement, often of a rotating or revolving body (e.g. the golfer).

$$\text{Angular velocity} = \frac{\text{Angular displacement}}{\text{Time}}$$

(°.s^{-1}) or (rad.$^{-1}$)

(Notice that 'speed' and 'distance' are together in one equation and 'velocity' and 'displacement' appear together in the other. Always keep vectors and scalars together!

Angular acceleration

This is the rate of change of angular velocity.

$$\text{Angular acceleration} = \frac{\text{Change in angular velocity}}{\text{Time}}$$

(°s^{-2}) or (rad.s^{-2})

or

$$\bar{\alpha} = \frac{wf - wi}{t}$$

where

$\bar{\alpha}$ = average angular acceleration

wf = final angular velocity

wi = initial angular velocity

t = time

Angular motion – torque, moment and levers

> *The turning effect produced by the application of a force.*

Torque/moment

The **torque/moment** may be defined as the *turning effect* of a force. The terms 'torque' and 'moment' are used synonymously because they have the same meaning.

> To calculate a torque/moment, it requires the multiplication of the *force* and the *perpendicular distance* between the line of action of the force and the axis/pivot.

> Example: if we have a force (F) acting as shown with a pivot (p), the torque/moment would be F x *d* = F*d* (Nm) clockwise.

[Nm = Newton metres]

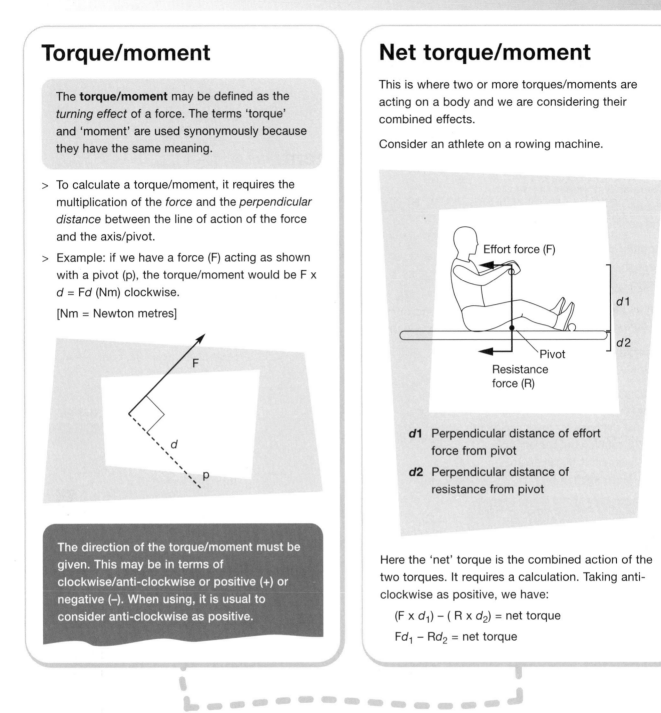

The direction of the torque/moment must be given. This may be in terms of clockwise/anti-clockwise or positive (+) or negative (–). When using, it is usual to consider anti-clockwise as positive.

Net torque/moment

This is where two or more torques/moments are acting on a body and we are considering their combined effects.

Consider an athlete on a rowing machine.

*d*1 Perpendicular distance of effort force from pivot

*d*2 Perpendicular distance of resistance from pivot

Here the 'net' torque is the combined action of the two torques. It requires a calculation. Taking anti-clockwise as positive, we have:

$$(F \times d_1) - (R \times d_2) = \text{net torque}$$

$$Fd_1 - Rd_2 = \text{net torque}$$

A lever is a rigid structure with a pivot point (fulcrum) and two opposing forces acting at two other points.

Levers in the body system may be considered as bones (rigid structure), joints (pivot/fulcrum), effort force (muscle insertion) and resistance force (load).

> Levers are designed to:
  – increase the amount of resistance that can be overcome by a force
  – increase the speed and range of movement of the resistance.
> If the effort arm is greater than the resistance arm, it will be easier to move the resistance because the effort torque will be greater.
> If the resistance arm is greater than the effort arm, the speed and range of movement of the resistance is increased.

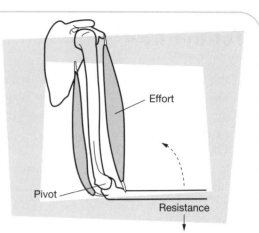

Effort arm = perpendicular distance between pivot and line of action of effort force.

Resistance arm/Load = perpendicular distance between pivot and line of action of resistance force.

Classes of lever

1 First class

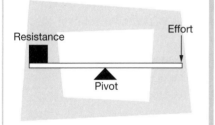

Here, the pivot is in between the resistance and effort ('seesaw' set up).

Example: nodding action of head. The neck muscles provide the effort, the skull/vertebra joint is the fulcrum/pivot and the weight of the head is the resistance.

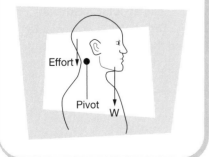

2 Second class

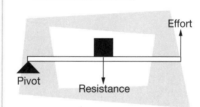

Notice that this arrangement mechanically favours effort at the expense of speed and range of movement of resistance.

Here, the pivot is at one end with the resistance in the middle (like a wheelbarrow).

Example: foot – ball of foot is fulcrum/pivot; weight of body acting through lower leg is the resistance; and the effort is the gastrocnemius (calf) acting through the Achilles tendon.

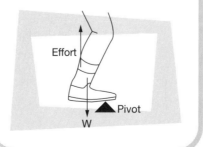

3 Third class

Notice that this arrangement mechanically favours resistance, but potentially we have greater speed and range of movement.

Here, the effort is in the middle and the pivot and resistance at either end.

Example: biceps acting on elbow joint. Pivot is elbow joint; effort is biceps acting through tendon; and resistance the weight of forearm. This is the most common lever system in the body.

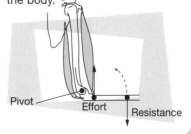

Angular motion – generating rotation

> *Adjusting the point of application of a force to produce rotation.*

Rotation is an angular movement; translation is a linear movement.

Eccentric force

Consider a gymnast applying a force (*F*) to a gymnastics box in order to move it in the horizontal plane.

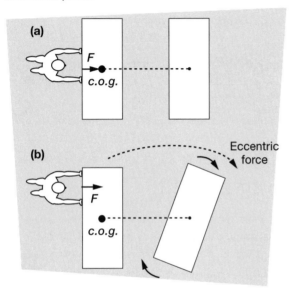

In diagram (a), because the force (*F*) is through the centre of gravity (c.o.g.) of the box, we get movement in a straight line – TRANSLATION.

In diagram (b), because the force (*F*) is 'off line' with the centre of gravity we get some linear motion (translation) and some angular motion (ROTATION).

> Any force that causes or tends to cause translation and rotation is called an eccentric force.

It is often the ground reaction force that acts as the force eccentric to the athlete's centre of gravity.

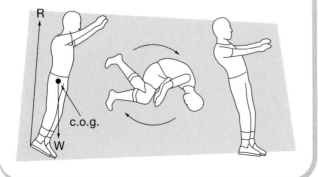

Couple

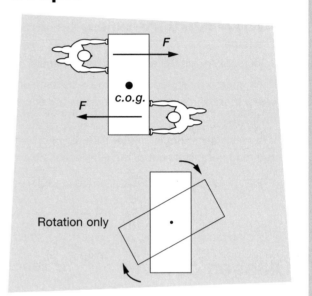

If the two gymnasts apply an equal force (*F*) an equal distance from the centre of gravity, this is known as a **couple**. This will produce rotation only.

> Therefore a couple may be defined as 'a system of two parallel, equal and opposite eccentric forces acting on an object'.

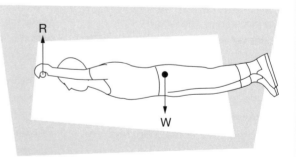

Here, the gymnast is rotating about a 'fixed' bar producing rotation only. The couple is produced by the weight force (W) and the reaction force (R) of the hand contact.

Fluid mechanics – water

> *The movement of a body through water.*

We now consider what happens to a body as it moves through water.

> What forces act on it?

> How does the body float?

> How can a swimmer reduce the drag effect?

Centre of buoyancy

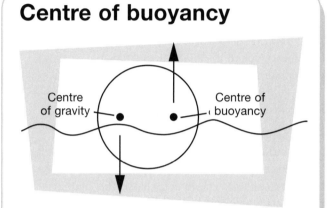

Centre of gravity

Centre of buoyancy

> A body will only be stable in the water when the centre of gravity is in line with the **centre of buoyancy**.

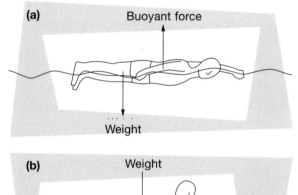

(a)

Buoyant force

Weight

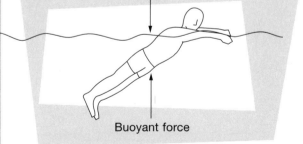

(b)

Weight

Buoyant force

In position (a) the swimmer is unstable until the weight and the buoyant force are in line (b).

Flotation

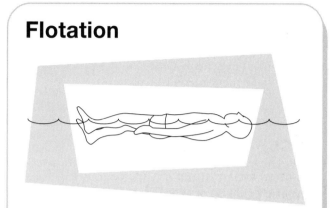

> A body will float if the weight of the body ≤ the maximum buoyant force.

The buoyant force is equal to the weight of the water displaced by an object. This is known as the **Archimedes' principle**.

Drag and lift

> The swimmer will need to reduce the cross-sectional area of the body by adopting a 'flat' position in the water. This will reduce drag.

> Surface drag (skin friction) may be reduced by shaving the body or using special costumes.

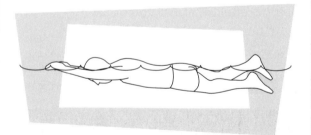

> In the same way an 'angle of attack' generates lift for a discus. Angling the hand as it moves sideways in the 'pull' phase may also generate lift. If angled correctly, this may have a forward component.

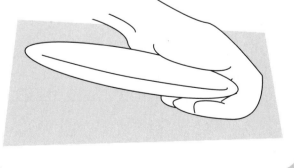

Angular analogues of Newton's Laws of Motion

> *Applying Newton's Laws of Motion to generate rotation.*

If something is an 'analogue' of something else the two things are similar to each other in some way. The following are the angular motion equivalents to the linear motion laws (see page 76).

Newton's First Law

> A body will continue to rotate with constant angular momentum unless an external torque is applied.

(Notice that with angular motion we are dealing with rotational movement and not linear motion or torques).

> Here, angular momentum refers to the *amount* of angular motion.

> With linear momentum we calculate by multiplying mass by velocity.

  Momentum = Mass (kg) x Velocity (ms^{-1})

> But with angular momentum we multiply the moment of inertia (distribution of mass about the axis of rotation) by the angular velocity.

  Angular momentum =
  Moment of inertia x Angular velocity (kg.m^2.s^{-1})

Now let us look at the interplay of angular momentum, angular velocity and moment of inertia. Consider a gymnast performing a back somersault – flight phase only!

At the beginning ❶, the gymnast has an extended body position. This gives the gymnast a high moment of inertia (mass distributed away from axis of rotation the transverse axis passing through hips). This produces slow rotation (low angular velocity).

At ❷, the mass has been brought closest to the axis of rotation. This results in a reduction of the moment of inertia and therefore an increase in the angular velocity.

At ❸, the gymnast is 'opening' out and extending again, increasing the moment of inertia and reducing the angular velocity.

Notice that angular momentum remains constant throughout the flight as no external torque is acting due to absence of ground reaction.

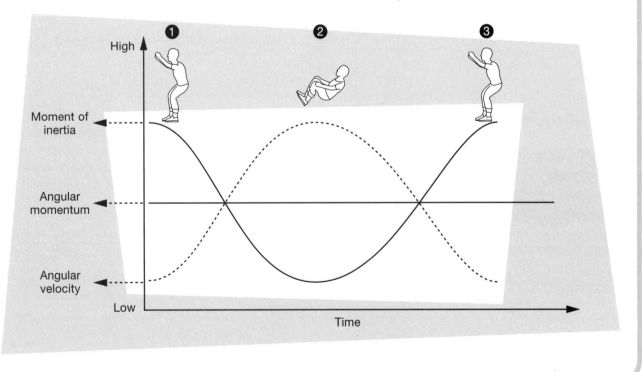

Newton's Second Law

> The rate of change of angular momentum is proportional to the external torque applied and acts in the direction of the applied torque.
>
> +
>
> The change of angular momentum is directly proportional to the length of time that the torque is applied.

Consider a gymnast about to perform a back somersault.

In order to get a large change of angular momentum, the torque needs to be applied for a long period of time. This requires contact with the ground for as long as possible. This is achieved by fully extending hip, knee and ankle joints prior to take off ❹.

This relates to angular impulse
(i.e. Angular impulse = Torque x Time).

Torque generated by ground reaction force

Newton's Third Law

> For every action torque exerted by one body on another, there is an equal but opposite reaction torque.

Consider a gymnast performing a 'pike' action.

Here, an equal and opposite torque is applied to each half of the gymnast's body.

Fluid mechanics – air

> *The movement of a body through air.*

In this section we will consider what happens to a ball as it moves through the air.

> What forces act on it?
> What makes a cricket ball swing as it moves through the air after leaving the bowler's arm?
> Why do golf balls have 'dimples'?
> Why does a tennis player put 'top spin' on a tennis ball?

Air flow

Consider a ball moving through the air:

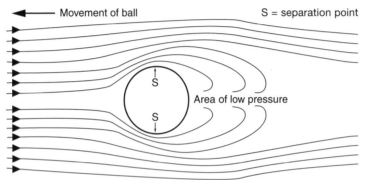

Movement of ball   S = separation point

Area of low pressure

> As the flow lines of the air hit the front of the ball, those closest to the ball's surface compress and move quicker.

> Once the flow lines reach S they change from *laminar* flow to *turbulent* flow. This creates an area of low pressure behind the ball. This results in a force from front to back acting to slow the ball down. This force is known as **profile** or **form drag**.

> As the ball travels faster, the separation point S moves forward (up to a *critical velocity*). This results in greater turbulent flow behind the ball, lower pressure and therefore increased profile drag.

> A larger cross-sectional area will also produce more turbulent flow and increase form drag.

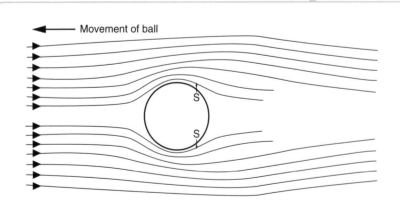

Movement of ball

Note: the layer closest to the ball is called the boundary layer.

> As the ball moves faster, it reaches a critical velocity. (This changes with ball size and surface characteristics.) This results in a

later separation point, less turbulence and therefore increases pressure behind the ball. This means less profile drag. (The late separation point is caused by the boundary layer becoming turbulent and 'sticking' to the surface of the ball.)

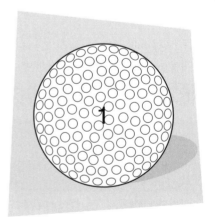

> Golf balls have dimples to 'trip' the boundary layer into turbulent flow at lower velocities therefore reducing profile drag and increasing distance.

Surface characteristics

Here we can see a cricket ball with an angled seam. When the air flow meets the seam early on (left), the boundary layer is 'tripped' into turbulent flow and 'sticks' to the ball. This pulls the other flow lines in and creates a lower pressure on the left-hand side – thus the ball will swing from right to left.

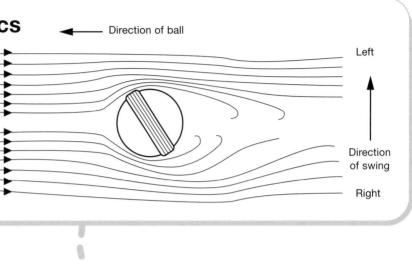

Direction of ball

Left

Direction of swing

Right

Spin

> Here we have a tennis ball hit with 'top spin'. This results in the 'compression' of flow lines below the ball. Whenever you get a compression of flow lines, the pressure is reduced (Bernoulli effect). Therefore there will be a 'net' force acting down (Magnus effect).

> The Magnus effect can also be seen in golf when the ball is 'hooked' or 'sliced'. Here, the effect is on horizontal motion.

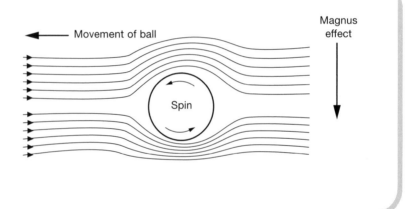

Movement of ball

Magnus effect

Spin

Lift

> The aerofoil makes use of the Bernoulli effect (compression of flow lines).

> Here the lines on the top of the aerofoil are compressed and produce a low pressure area. This produces a 'net' upward lift force.

This is the principle behind the design of aircraft wings!

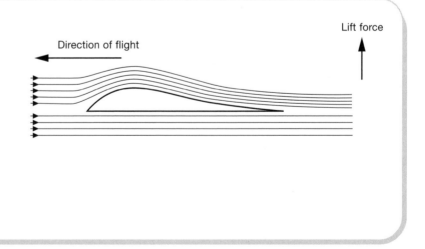

Direction of flight

Lift force

Individual differences (1)

> *That which makes us what we are.*

Personality

Either

The sum total of an individual's characteristics which makes him or her unique.

Or

The overall pattern of psychological characteristics that makes each person unique.

Measuring personality

Measuring personality is thought to be useful for predicting behaviour which may help identify top-class performers from an early age. But there are problems in ensuring validity and reliability. All techniques may be time consuming and costly and the interpretation of results may cause over-generalisation, particularly if small numbers are used.

Methods include:

Interviews (e.g. Rorschach inkblot) but...

> are they reliable and valid in each case?
> are they of value in assessing a person's sporting ability?

Questionnaires (e.g. personality tests, Minnesota multiphasic personality inventory, Cattell 16 primary factors questionnaire)

> are these appropriate for the results the researcher wants?

Observation

> difficult to remain unobtrusive which will affect behaviour
> secret observation is unethical.

Personalities are formed, depending on the theory you follow.

Trait theories

Traits are relatively stable, highly consistent attributes that exert a widely generalised causal effect on behaviour (Mischel).

These are innate characteristics which can be arranged in a hierarchy, for example:

> outgoing
> aggressive
> tense
> shy
> relaxed
> sensitive

The strongest traits dominate the behaviour.

Situation does not play an important part in behaviour.

Eysenck's theory

Eysenck identified two main dimensions of personality. A person can fall anywhere along the two dimensions.

	unstable	
moody		tough
rigid		aggressive
pessimistic		excitable
unsociable		impulsive
quiet		active
introverted		*extroverted*
passive		sociable
thoughtful		outgoing
controlled		response
reliable	*stable*	lively
calm		leader

Narrow band approach

Personality seen as two contrasting types indicated by behaviour:

> **Type A** – highly strung, impatient, intolerant, high levels of stress
> **Type B** – relaxed, tolerant, low levels of personal stress

Sheldon's somatotyping personality formation

A form of trait theory (How true is this for everyone?)

Ectomorphy   tenseness
(Basil Fawlty type figure)

Mesomorphy   extrovert, risk taker
(sportsman figure)

Endomorphy   sociability, comfort loving
(Santa Claus figure)

Lewin's interactionist approach

This recognises that the trait approach and social learning approach together have value in determining behaviour

B = f (P . E)
Behaviour is the **F**unction of **P**ersonality and **E**nvironment

Personality characteristics predict some behaviour in some situations but not all situations.

Bandura's social learning theory

Personality is learnt by observational learning, modelling and imitating behaviour, and through experience. Psychological functioning occurs as a result of environmental determinants affecting behaviour.

Assertion/Aggression

Assertion (channelled aggression or instrumental aggression) is behaviour within the rules of the game that achieves a goal, e.g. tackling fairly but forcefully within a soccer match.

Aggression is the intention to harm another person outside the laws of a game, e.g. punching an opponent in a soccer match.

Some, not universally accepted theories suggest that aggression occurs as a result of:

> **natural instinct.** This theory has many detractors – cultural background often disproves this and aggression is often not spontaneous.
> **frustration.** This theory states that frustration always leads to aggression; a person is blocked from their goal, they are frustrated and release the tension through aggressive action. Berkowitz (1974) maintains that this can make a person 'potentially aggressive'.
> **social learning.** People see significant others (heroes) being aggressive and imitate this behaviour in similar situations (Bandura, 1977).

Combatting aggression

A mixture of recommendations, affecting performers, coaches, administrators and others, include:

> control of arousal levels (stress management)
> avoidance of situations that cause aggression
> stopping aggressive players from further participation
> rewarding 'turning the other cheek'
> showing non-aggressive role models
> punishing aggression
> reinforcement of non-aggression (largely by significant others)
> handing responsibility to an aggressive player.

Individual differences (2)

> *How we approach situations.*

Attitudes

A learned emotional and behavioural response to a stimulus or situation. Attitudes are often seen as an extension of personality.

Attitudes are formed from:

> pleasant or unpleasant experiences forming our approach to the same situation – soccer training made me ill last week; I don't like training.

> significant others (parents, teachers, friends) through encouragement, reward or punishment, or peer group pressure – soccer training is an excellent way to improve skills and all the best players do it.

Triadic Model

Attitudes are formed from three components:

cognitive reflect your belief in information, e.g. weight training increases muscle bulk (not necessarily true)

affective reflect your feelings or emotional response (a determined direction of behaviour), e.g. muscle bulk is good/bad

behavioral reflect your intended behaviour, e.g. I will/will not go weight training.

Also note...

Attitudes do not always predict behaviour, only specific attitudes predict specific behaviours. (Fishbein, 1995)

The best indicator of behaviour is an individual's behaviour intention. A positive attitude to something incorporates an intention to do that thing and therefore participation is more likely. (La Piere, 1934)

Changing attitudes

Persuasion

Three factors affect a person's ability to persuade another.

> The persuader must be of high status. He/she must be knowledgeable and appear genuine. Attractiveness and similarity to persuadee might be important.

> The message must be clear, concise and accurate. It may be best to put only one side of the argument, depending on the audience. The strongest argument first or last? This depends upon the proximity of expected change in behaviour.

> The people being persuaded must be capable of understanding the message. They may choose not to be persuaded.

Cognitive dissonance

If there is a mismatch in the Triadic Model, this will cause a dissonance (imbalance) in the mind of the person being persuaded. They must then act to reduce this imbalance by changing behaviour to meet new criteria, based on new information.

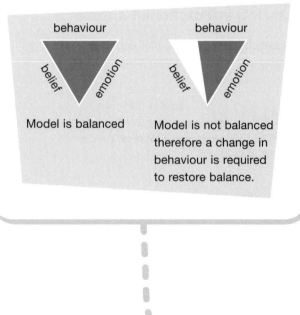

Model is balanced

Model is not balanced therefore a change in behaviour is required to restore balance.

Stress and anxiety (1)

> *Giving athletes an 'edge'.*

Stress

a stimulus resulting in arousal or a response to a specific situation.

Arousal

a state of readiness to perform that helps motivate individuals (see page 93).

Anxiety

a negative reaction of a performer to stress, often leading to over arousal.

Eustress

a positive reaction of a performer to stress, leading to optimal arousal.

Stress

Stressors

Stressors are situations that cause a stress response. In PE and sport the following are the most common:

> competition – an evaluative and comparative situation that increases anxiety

> conflict – with opponents or team mates who choose to do things differently

> frustration – can be caused if we are blocked from achieving our goals... aggression can result

> environmental conditions – extremes of heat or cold

> injury and fatigue – preventing effective performance.

Stress response

Seyle (1956) proposed the **General Adaptation Syndrome** model to explain how the body copes with stress.

Alarm reaction
Fight or flight reaction; adrenaline surge, increased heart rate, blood sugar level up.

Resistance
Body adapts to cope with new stress until it is removed or overcome.

Exhaustion
If stress is not removed the body begins to fail to cope with this stress, this may take weeks, months or even years.

Stress experience

Athletes experience psychological symptoms in addition to the physical symptoms described:

> inability to make decisions

> poor concentration

> feelings of worry

> narrowing attention.

These can lead to even more stress and the stress spiral:

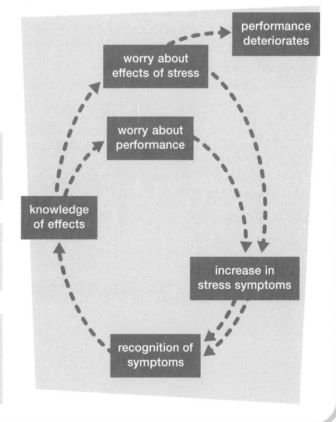

Stress and anxiety (2)

> *Our response to stress.*

Anxiety

> **Anxiety** – an emotional state, similar to fear, associated with arousal and accompanied by feelings of nervousness and apprehension.

> **State anxiety** – the athlete's emotional state at that particular time (the intensity of the response alters from time to time and situation to situation).

> **Trait anxiety** – the athlete's disposition to view any situation as threatening and to respond with heightened state anxiety levels.

Athletes with high trait anxiety levels tend to view all evaluative situations as threatening. They respond with greater intensity of state anxiety than those athletes with lower trait anxiety levels. Martens (1977) identified this trait anxiety as **competitive trait anxiety**.

Martens used a self-report questionnaire called **sports competition anxiety test** (SCAT) to find out how athletes felt prior to competitions. This has proved reliable for predicting anxiety levels in the future.

Measuring stress

This is achieved in three ways.

Self report questionnaires

Easily administered, but may not always give a truthful picture:

> Martens' sports competition anxiety test (SCAT)

> Speilberger's state trait anxiety inventory (STAI).

Physiological measurements

Often require bulky, expensive equipment and some of these measurements would be affected by exercise, before or afterwards, anyway:

> heart rates (ECG)

> temperature (thermometer)

> oxygen uptake (Douglas bag analysis)

> sweating (sudorimeter)

> skin conductivity (galvanic skin response)

> muscle tension (electromyogram).

Behavioural observation

Coaches should be able to build up a pattern of responses over an extended period, before, during and after training and competition. Changes they may see include:

> nail biting

> shaking

> rapid talking

> frequent visits to the toilet.

Stress management

> *Controlling our responses to stress.*

Stress management skills are vital for those athletes who want to become the very best. The ability to control anxiety at crucial times is very important. Both somatic and cognitive anxiety control is essential.

Physical relaxation

Progressive muscle relaxation

The progressive tensing of muscle groups and subsequent greater relaxation of these same muscles (often coach or teacher directed) – excellent preparation for imagery exercises.

Self directed relaxation

Similar to progressive muscle relaxation but without tensing muscles first – relies on the athlete's ability to isolate muscles and then relax them (this can be improved through practice).

Deep breathing

To focus the mind only on breathing – can reduce heart and respiration rates as well as calming the mind.

Biofeedback

Immediate visual feedback of physiological measures of stress (e.g. heart rate) allows the athlete to concentrate on reducing that measurement – they get immediate feedback of their success.

Imagery

Imagery is the creation of a mental picture to relax or prepare the athlete for activity. It comes in two forms:

> external – watching yourself perform, from outside your body

> internal – seeing your performance from your body (visualisation).

Imagery for relaxation often takes the athlete to comfortable surroundings, e.g. a favourite place, or a place to relax, a tropical desert island.

Imagery to prepare for activity often involves mental rehearsal of the skills to be attempted. Explanations for the success of imagery include:

> **neuromuscular** – thinking about action produces nerve impulses that fire in correct order (a dry run)

> **cognitive** – thinking through likely scenarios the performer is ready for them when they occur

> **confidence building** – athletes gain in confidence as they know what they are going to do which reduces anxiety and increases motivation.

Goal setting

Goal setting is useful for performers in the following ways:

> attention is directed and uncertainty reduced

> learning is focused

> practices are well structured; effort is organised to fulfil all tasks correctly

> confidence is increased (success comes more quickly)

> evaluation and feedback are immediate and focused.

Goal setting will be effective if the goals:

> are appropriately challenging
They may be just beyond the previous best performance – this generally improves motivation of the performer.

> have a long term vision
This will be approached via short and intermediate achievements. Short term goals allow success to be gained, increasing motivation for the long term goals.

> are measurable
Goals must be measurable to allow accurate feedback. The performer must know when they have arrived at a goal.

> suit both the coach and performer
Negotiation is the key. The performer will have greater motivation if they feel they have ownership of the goals.

Motivation – concepts and theories

> *An internal factor that arouses and directs behaviour.*

It is suggested (Sage, 1974) that motivation is a combination of "The internal mechanisms and external stimuli which arouse and direct behaviour."

Intrinsic motivation

All suggested by Hull's 'Drive Theory'.

The performer:

> may possess the desire to overcome a particular problem or task

> develops skills or 'habits' to overcome that problem

> practises successful habits until perfected

> attains a feeling of pride, satisfaction, joy and fun in completing the task which is rewarding – motivation is enhanced

> then sets a new goal or task to continue with the drive or motivation to succeed.

The teacher/coach, to facilitate the performer's intrinsic motivation:

> aims for success with the performer

> ensures that practice and training are enjoyable

> uses a varied approach to maintain interest.

Extrinsic motivation

These are rewards that are external to the performer and fall into two categories.

Tangible rewards
> medals
> trophies
> money etc.

Intangible rewards
> praise from significant others
> recognition etc.

Fantastic!

COACH

Teachers and coaches should ensure that they praise desired behaviour as this motivates individuals to repeat it. However, the use of tangible rewards, particularly with young children, should be limited as it (and not play) may become the sole reason for performance.

Goal setting

Well thought out and motivating goals must be:

S > specific
M > measurable
A > agreed
R > realistic
T > time related
E > exciting
R > recorded

Athletes require a mixture of intrinsic and extrinsic motivation, with well planned goals to **achieve success.**

Motivation:

> involves our inner ambition to achieve our aims

> depends upon external stressors and or rewards for our efforts

> is related to the intensity (arousal level) and direction of behaviour.

For success – these three factors must be kept in balance.

Good coaches manipulate performers' levels of motivation to maximise performance. Performance and motivation are closely linked to arousal and performance.

Two theories explain the relationship between arousal and performance.

Hull's Drive Theory

A linear relationship between performance and arousal.

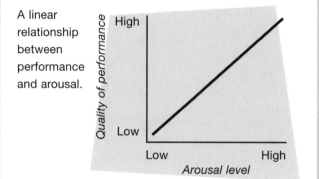

This theory helps explain *why beginners find it difficult to perform well under pressure*. Often beginners' skill level decreases if they are competing in a relay race using new skills – for example in a football dribbling race.

However it also explains *how experienced athletes perform better when under pressure* using well learned skills – for example when good tennis players play better against stronger opposition.

Performance = habit x drive

Novices have usually incorrect habits. Experts have well-learned correct habits.

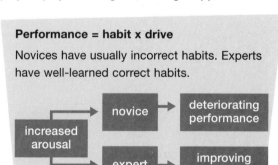

Habit is the performance that is strongest in that person (not always the correct performance) usually the one that occurs most in practice.

Drive is the level of arousal.

Yerkes Dodson or Inverted 'U' Law

An increase in arousal causes improvement in performance up to an optimal point. After this point, increased arousal leads to deteriorated performance.

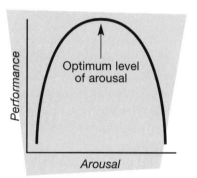

Three factors affect the application of this theory in every case:

> **activity undertaken**

Fine movements and complex skills (which require large amounts of attention) require a lower arousal level, e.g. snooker safety shots, pistol shooting, etc.

> **skill levels**

Highly skilled athletes, with well-learned motor programmes, have spare attention capacity to deal with excessive arousal. Beginners need all of their attention to be focused on the skill and do not cope with over arousal so well.

> **personality**

Generally extroverts perform better with high arousal levels and introverts perform better with low arousal levels. This is linked to a part of the brain called the reticular activating system (RAS) which controls the level of arousal. Introverts have highly stimulated RAS; they avoid situations that will increase their already high levels of arousal. Extroverts need high arousal situations to stimulate RAS.

Motivation – personality and experience

> *Improving performances.*

What motivates the drive for achievement? Why do some people choose to undertake a particular challenge and others decline?

Three influences play major roles. They help explain why some people perform well in difficult situations (and seem to enjoy the experience)

and why some people never take up new challenges. Good coaches understand this concept.

The influence of personality

> Some people display 'approach behaviour'; they seem to thrive on challenge and possess a need to achieve (NACH).

> Others display avoidance behaviours and try to avoid challenges because they have a need to avoid failure (NAF).

These behaviours occur most readily in judgemental situations. Sport can be very judgemental, comparing two performances, thus it is said that sport attracts more 'NACH' personalities than 'NAF' personalities.

NACH personalities:

> are determined to see a task through

> work quickly at a task

> take risks

> enjoy a challenge

> take responsibility

> like to know how they have been judged.

E.g. sportsmen/women, games players, climbers

NAF personalities:

> are easily dissuaded from taking the challenge

> work at tasks slowly or not at all

> avoid situations where they or their ego is put at risk

> avoid responsibility

> prefer not to be judged and do not want to know how they have been judged.

E.g. those who play only against weaker players

Ego oriented

Athletes who view success as defeating an opponent and thus being seen as a greater player, e.g. players of games such as chess or combat sports performers.

Task oriented

Athletes who view success as an internal achievement, e.g. runners beating their personal best or climbers completing a more difficult route.

Knowing what motivates athletes helps coaches/teachers to plan training sessions for them.

The influence of self-confidence

Bandura (1977) identified a specific form of self-confidence which he called self-efficacy. Bandura claims that this type of self confidence varies from situation to situation.

Athletes will choose to participate in activities in which they have high self-efficacy and avoid situations in which they don't have high self-efficacy. Self-efficacy affects our effort in an activity and our persistence at a task.

Self-efficacy is affected by four factors:

> **Performance accomplishments**

  The biggest influence on self-efficacy is the recognition of past achievements and the attributions given for successes. Controllable internal factors are likely to ensure feelings of self-confidence.

> **Vicarious experiences (modelling)**

  Seeing a task successfully completed, particularly by

The influence of experience

How an athlete has performed in the past will affect how they approach the next challenge. Athletes will look for reasons for their past performances – good or bad.

event outcome – win/loss/ success/ failure

information about performance available to athlete

attribution of the causes of the performance

expectation of future performance

affective response – how you feel

decision on future participation

Weiner (1974) looked at examination performance and candidates' attitudes. He was able to make a two-dimensional model (a).

This is a good model for examinations but is not always applicable in sports specific situations. Roberts and Pascuzzi (1979) enhanced the model (b).

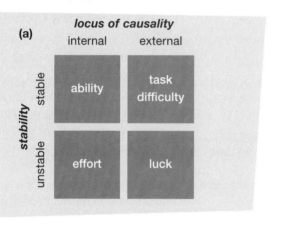

(a)

locus of causality

	internal	external
stable	ability	task difficulty
unstable	effort	luck

stability

(b)

locus of causality

	internal	external
stable	ability	coaching
unstable	> effort > unstable ability > behavioral factors > practice	> luck > task difficulty > teamwork > officials

stability

Learned helplessness (Dweck 1978)

This is the belief that failure is inevitable in specific situations... or in some cases in all situations. This leads to feelings of helplessness. Attribution to uncontrollable factors often leads to learned helplessness.

> Success is often attributed to internal causes – "I played well today and won well."

> Failure is often attributed to external factors – "He got a few lucky breaks on crucial points."

This is known as a 'self serving bias' and protects or enhances a performer's ego.

someone of a similar standard, helps raise a performers self-confidence.

> **Verbal persuasion**

Significant others can help reluctant performers begin to believe that they can accomplish the task ahead.

> **Emotional arousal**

If a performer feels they are in control of their arousal levels through management techniques, or due to their own ability, they will have greater self-efficacy.

In practice these factors can help athletes low in confidence to achieve. They, or their coaches, can:

> ensure success by setting achievable goals and highlighting past success

> demonstrate techniques with a peer as the model

> encourage persuasion and support from friends and others

> use relaxation techniques as a part of the athlete's training programme.

Social influences on performances

> *Watching others and learning.*

Socialisation

Socialisation is the acquisition by children of the norms of society: expected behaviours, values, rights and wrongs, and rules and status. Children acquire these qualities by observing others and imitating them. This is observational learning or modelling.

Physical education plays a vital roll in the socialisation of all children in all aspects of sports participation.

In physical education it is normally not possible to use powerful or famous role models in lessons.

Research (Landers & Landers, 1973) has shown that careful use of demonstration is vital if success is to be achieved. All groups observing models improved their performance compared with a control group who saw no models.

> Performances improved most when demonstration was by a **skilled teacher**.
> The least amount of improvement was by the group with an **unskilled teacher**.
> A demonstration by **unskilled peers** proved to be the second most effective model.
> **Skilled peers** produced improvements only slightly better than an unskilled teacher.

Bandura's (1961) work on modelling identified seven important considerations in the use of models relative to young people.

> Appropriate behaviour to social norms is more likely to be copied – boys will imitate assertive rugby play if it is modelled by male rugby players.
> Young people will imitate behaviour only if they see it as relevant to them – soccer players may not imitate assertive rugby play as it is not relevant to them.
> Role models who are similar to the pupils are more likely to be copied – peers who perform skills well may elicit more accurate imitation than older (professional) sportsmen.
> Encouraging and approachable models – teachers who listen to young people, who are supportive and helpful – are more likely to be copied.
> Powerful role models are more likely to be copied – a much respected performer is more likely to be imitated than a local (unknown) sportsman.
> Models whose behaviour is condoned by significant others (parents, peers, teachers) are more likely to be copied – telling a young person "I want you to go out and perform like Alan Shearer today" may encourage the young person to work hard for the team but it may also encourage them to be very assertive in their play.
> Behaviour that is consistent is more likely to be imitated – if a normally calm player shows dissent on rare occasions this is unlikely to be copied as it would be inconsistent with his normal actions.

Bandura developed his work and in 1977 established a model to demonstrate the effect of demonstration on skill learning.

acquisition			*performance*		
observation	attention	retention	motor reproduction	motivation	performance
The observer will watch the model perform skills.	The observer will pay particular attention to the cues for the skills – attractiveness and status of the model will affect this.	The observer must create a mental picture of the performance – mental rehearsal will be beneficial.	The observer must be physically capable of performing the skill and will attempt to match their performance to that of the model – the model performance must be a perfect demonstration.	The observer's motivation must be at the correct level. They must want to copy the model's performance – this may need help and reinforcement from a coach.	The observer copies what they have watched.

Questions arose from the findings...

> Do unskilled teachers inhibit learning because students don't want to show them up?
> Do unsuccessful demonstrations by unskilled teachers make students believe they will fail?

> Do unskilled peers set up a competitive standard that others try to beat?
> Should teachers only demonstrate if able to perform correctly – otherwise use peers?

Social facilitation

> How does the crowd or audience affect behaviour?

The influence of the presence of others on performance (Zajonc, 1965).

Alone or with others?

The presence of others creates a powerful social influence on performers due to **social evaluation** – even when this is not overt.

Performers can suffer from **evaluation apprehension** in this situation; this creates increased arousal levels, especially if the audience is made up of significant others for the performer.

In front of a crowd?

Facilitation implies performance improvement due to the presence of audience... but this is not always the case. Evidence points to a poorer performance when an audience is present in some cases.

Evidence suggests that the presence of others increases arousal level, indicated by increased palm sweating, increased heart rate, and that performance is linked to drive theory (page 93).

Four points have been raised:
> presence of audience or co-actors increases arousal or drive
> increased arousal will increase likelihood of dominant response occurring
> if the skill is well learned the response will be correct
> if the skill is not well learned the response will be incorrect.

In front of a 'home' crowd?

A 'home' crowd is more likely to contain significant others and therefore more likely to evaluate a performance. For some athletes this causes increased evaluation apprehension arousal which can lead to poorer performances depending on their skill level, personality (type 'A' person play less well in front of an audience) and previous performances.

However, most research suggests an advantage of playing in front of friendly home support which seems to encourage adventurous attacking play and solid defence.

Martens (1969) found:
> in *learning* complex skills, individuals learned skills better if they were alone
> in *performing* complex skills individuals performed well learned skills better if they had an audience.

The relationship between performance and arousal is crucial and the effect of the presence of others can make control of arousal level more difficult.

Can behaviour be changed?

Performers and coaches work on ways to cope with the negative effects of social facilitation.

Advice includes:
> use relaxation techniques (see page 91)
> use mental imagery to block out audience
> teach new skills in a non-evaluative way
> explain to athletes how audiences are likely to affect them
> encourage a supportive atmosphere amongst team members.

Groups and teams

> More than the sum of the individuals?

Definitions

> A **team** is... two or more persons interacting with one another, influencing each other (Shaw, 1976).

> A **group** has... a collective identity, sharing a common purpose, with structured communication patterns (Carron, 1980).

> **Cohesion** is... the reason why a group of people come together, and the resistance of the members of the group to its break-up.

Does cohesion facilitate improved performance?

Teams with high task cohesion have a greater potential for success than teams who are more socially cohesive. Teams in sports that require greater interaction, e.g. basketball, need greater cohesion than teams where less interaction is required, e.g. swimming or judo.

Why join a team?

Members join teams or groups for two reasons. (Although usually a combination of both motives is common.)

Either

> They want to join a successful team in order to achieve success. This is a task oriented cohesion; all members of the team have the same goal. For example, amateur soccer players leaving one club to join another more successful club at the end of each season.

Or

> People join a team because they perceive that the group has good interpersonal relationships; they appear to enjoy each others' company no matter the result of matches. For example, amateur soccer players who remain with a club despite poor results because they share similar values, attitudes and enjoy the company of the players in that club.

Group performance

How to ensure that a team of individuals produce the best team performance?

Steiner (1972) produced a model to show the relationship between the performance of the team and the individuals.

$$\text{actual productivity} = \text{best potential productivity} - \text{losses due to faulty processes}$$

'Faulty' processes fall into two categories:

> **co-ordination problems**

  Strategies and tactics involving team mates working together with good timing and co-ordination may not work because individuals do not match up with each other on the day, e.g. a mistimed pass, a fumbled ball, a poor lineout in rugby.

> **motivational problems**

  Groups tend to make individuals perform below their own best potential.

> **The Ringlemann effect** – experiments have shown that teams of eight (say, tug-of-war) do not work eight times better than eight individuals; some team members lose their motivation in a team.

> **Social loafing** – team players lose motivation as they feel their contribution is not visible and therefore not valued. Records of 'assists' or passes made can counteract this... and socially cohesive teams suffer less in this respect.

Leadership

The behaviourial processes influencing individuals and groups towards set goals (Barrow, 1977). Leadership involves personal relationships and affects the motivation of individuals and groups.

Trait theory – leaders are born with leadership qualities (the 'Great Man' theory), e.g. Churchill, Alexander the Great, Caesar, etc.

Social learning theory – leaders learn to use their qualities to match the situation requirements, i.e. they treat subordinates in whatever way achieves their goals.

> Leaders tend to occur in two ways (Carron, 1981). They either:
>
> > **emerge** from within a group by consent of others or because of their talents, or
>
> > they are prescribed or **appointed** by an external source, e.g. manager, teacher, coach.

Leadership qualities

> ability to communicate
> enthusiasm
> high motivation
> a vision of what needs to be done
> high ability
> inspirational qualities – charisma.

Leadership styles

Two broad types of leaders occur... although most effective leaders are a mixture of both:

> **task oriented** – concerned mainly with the demands of the task

> **person oriented** – concerned mainly with interpersonal relationships within a group.

Classically the following continuum is suggested:

Authoritarian	Democratic	Laissez-faire
Task oriented, dictatorial in style, makes all decisions, commanding, direct approach.	Person oriented, values the group's view, shares decisions, shows interest in others.	Makes few decisions, gives little feedback to group members who do as they wish.

Leadership categories

(Chelladurai, 1978)

> training and behaviour – usually improves performance
> democratic behaviour – decisions made together
> autocratic behaviour – authoritarian
> social support – concern for individuals behaviour
> rewarding behaviour – giving positive feedback

Good leaders use all five behaviours as the situation demands. Effective leadership will occur when all of the demands of the situation are satisfied, i.e.

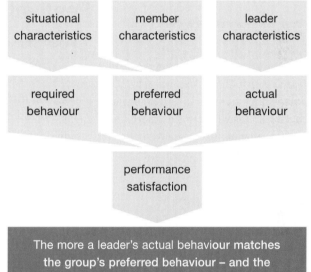

situational characteristics	member characteristics	leader characteristics
required behaviour	preferred behaviour	actual behaviour

performance satisfaction

> The more a leader's actual behaviour matches the group's preferred behaviour – and the required behaviour of the situation – the more effective the leadership.

Fiedler (1967) suggests that a leader's effectiveness relies upon whether they are task or person oriented and the situation.

Task oriented leaders are most effective when the situation is either *most* favourable and *least* favourable, e.g. in a very dangerous situation or in a situation where demotivation is likely due to ease of task.

Person oriented leaders are most effective in moderately favourable conditions.

Festivals... and blood sports

> *Local holidays provided time for enjoyment.*

communal time off work with chattering, eating, drinking, singing, dancing, betting

Parish feasts

> sometimes called wakes or revels
> celebrated around religious (e.g. patron saints, Whitsun) or seasonal events (e.g. harvest, shearing)

Rural games

> linked to seasonal work
> a chance to display skill and strength

Fairs

> once or twice a year
> linked to the farming calendar
> labourers advertised their skills
> farmers hire workers

Festival games

> **Single sticks** – winner was first to draw blood on an opponents head
> **Jingling matches** – blindfolded participants try to catch person with a bell around their neck
> **Whistling matches** – a 'Merry Andrew' pulls faces at whistlers. The winner is the participant who whistles for the longest without laughing
> **Smock racing** – women race for the prize of a dress

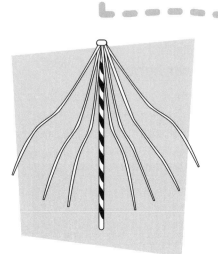

... and the blood sports

> **Cock fighting** – cocks, penned in by crowd, or in a pit, fought to the death; a big betting event.
> **Throwing at cocks** – passers-by paid to throw sticks or stones at a tethered bird; the thrower who killed it kept it.
> **Bull baiting** – bulldog attacked bull, trying to attach to its underside; the bull tossed the dogs who were caught by owners and sent back in (there was a general belief that this improved the meat).
> **Bear baiting** – dogs let loose on tethered bear causing the bear to rear up and make lots of noise (bears were not usually killed as they were expensive).
> **Dog fighting** – dogs, bred for their strength and speed, were used in noisy and viscious spectacles.

The spectators

The harsh living conditions of most people meant they had little pity when it came to the suffering of animals. Crowds were often violent, drunken and excitable. The events were a form of catharsis.

Field sports

> *Field sports offered different things to different parts of the community.*

Until relatively recently (the 1930s), the majority of the nation's population lived in the countryside. Thus field sports played an important part in their life. Hunting served two main purposes – food and recreation.

For the poor, hunting for food was a necessity, to feed the family. They were either involved in employment to feed the wealthy or in poaching (stealing animals from other people's property).

The wealthy, on the other hand, often hunted for leisure. This allowed them to show off their athleticism, to challenge themselves physically and to enjoy a social occasion.

Dissenting voices

Some people did not support hunting for pleasure. One person described it as a sport "that owes its pleasure to another's pain".

Fishing

> Fishing began in the mists of time when people needed to catch fish to live. No one knows exactly how long ago it all started but bone hooks have been found that date back 50000 years.

> Also known as angling, there are three types of fishing:
> – sea fishing
> – game fishing (e.g. salmon and trout)
> – coarse fishing (e.g. roach and bream in rivers, canals and lakes).

Fox hunting

> The fox was considered a vermin and hunting it was considered an exciting way of controlling a pest.

> Leaping over ditches and hedges on horseback required a great deal of skill.

> Breeding good horses and hounds was expensive.

> The ceremony around the sport appealed to the gentry (upper classes).

Falconry

> The aristocracy spent a good deal of time and resources breeding hunting birds.

> The skill was mastering the savage nature of the birds and creating a beautiful yet deadly hunter.

> The hunt was either by foot or on horseback.

Deer hunting

> Deer were considered to be vermin because they ate vegetation and trampled down fences.

> Deer were hunted with staghounds.

Ottering

> Dogs were used to track down and corner otters.

> Otters were then killed using long poles with forked ends.

> They were considered vermin because they depleted fish stocks.

Boar hunting

> Boars were hunted to extinction in Britain.

> They were pursued by dogs, and men on foot or horseback.

Fowling

Not a nasty tackle in soccer! A fowl is a bird, especially one that is hunted or that can be eaten as food (e.g. duck or chicken). So fowling is hunting these birds, with the intention of shooting them.

Games

> *Three examples of early English games.*

Both the rich and the poor played games. The characteristics of each class were reflected in the games they played.

The rich

> Plenty of leisure time
> Etiquette
> Sophisticated
> Nice facilities
> Played to rules
> Tactics involved
> Gambling on outcome

The poor

> Played only occasionally
> Often violent
> Drinking alcohol often part of the ritual
> No pitches or courts
> Few rules, easy for uneducated to understand
> Few, if any tactics
> Gambling on outcome

Cricket

> Where this game derived from has caused a great deal of debate. It is thought to be a hybrid of several games. Two of the most likely are 'cat and dog' and 'stool ball'. The first was an ancient Scottish game where the batsman guarded a hole in the ground. The latter originates from France and used a three-legged stool.

> Cricket was enjoyed by all sections of society. It could be played on the rough village wicket with a minimum of equipment, or in the fine setting of a country property.

> The gentry could play in the same team as the working class, but both sections had clearly defined roles. The former dictated tactics, the latter chased after the ball.

Tennis

> This is said to have been a game first enjoyed by the ancient Egyptians. But in the form we know it, it is derived from the French nobility.

> In the early days of 'real tennis' it was played without rackets. In France it was called 'jeu de paume' (game with the palm).

> Rackets were introduced to impart more spin and power to the ball.

> The indoor courts were a similar shape to modern courts. They were, however, expensive to build.

> The rules were complicated.

> The servants of the wealthy saw this game and derived their own version. This was often played in the courtyards of local pubs. This was convenient as it provided competitors, spectators, drink and a chance to gamble.

Mob football

> This was played all over England in various forms. Local conditions and customs gave rise to a large variety of games: Derby Mob Football, The Haxey Hood, The Halletan Bottle Game and Ashbourne Football are all examples.

> The general aim was to overcome your opponent by invading their territory or by dragging some piece of equipment into yours.

> This task was violently pursued and often caused injury.

> There were few rules. The number of competitors varied a great deal. Drinking was often part of the ritual.

> It was a game played by the lower classes and despised by the wealthy. The wealthy were worried that their property would be destroyed by the violent games.

> 'Mob football' was banned for the first time in 1314, during the reign of King Edward II. This did not stop it being played.

Combat sports

> *Modern day combat sports are boxing, karate, judo.*

These are sports that were taken from methods of protecting yourself. Gradually, rules and regulations were laid down, allowing combatants to pit their strength and skill against one another.

Archery

> The bow and arrow were the traditional weapon of peasants (used for hunting).
> After the Battle of Crecy (1346), when the British longbow won the day, the government decided all sports and pastimes should be stopped, except archery.
> The 17th century saw the development of firearms. Archery declined. Gradually became a refined sport for the upper and middle classes.
> It became codified with clubs, rules and ethics.

Jousting

> This appeared in various formats. It originated from the jousting tournaments of medieval knights. It was copied and from it quintain was developed. (The quintain was usually an object mounted on a post or support, set up as a mark to be tilted at with lances or poles. You could also throw darts or hoops at the quintain – as an exercise of skill.)
> The poor also had their own form on hobby horses or on small, unsteady boats.

Fencing

> The sword was the traditional weapon of the nobility.
> In the 17th century the sword was superseded by the gun. Instead, sword fighting developed into a sport and rules were drawn up for competing.
> Lower classes mimicked it with single sticks.

Wrestling

> Various types around the country. Each had its own rules and conventions (e.g. Devon and Cornwall; Cumberland and Westmoreland).
> Rural link: it was a way of demonstrating strength by local farm hands and often took place at country fairs.

Prize fighting

> Dates back to the 13th century where nobles learnt how to defend themselves.
> The nobility organised fights. For example, in 1681 the Duke of Albemarle set one up between his butcher and butler. We don't know what the prize was!

> Gradually the sport became more organised:
    1743 James Broughton's rules
    1857 Queensbury rules
> The former standardised fighting, but it was not until 1857 that it became more respectable and looked upon as a sport.
> Upper-class spectators; lower-class participants.

Social scene

> *How people lived.*

This is a snapshot of the social scene in Britain – as it was pre-industrial revolution. The panel provides a summary of the characteristics of popular recreation in times past.

Feudal
Gentry owned land – peasants worked for little return.

Rural
Majority of population lived and worked in the country.

Small communities
Everyone knew everyone in your community.

Literacy
Poor: mostly illiterate. Worked from a very young age.

Wealthy: generally literate.

Work
Poor: worked long hours. The work was:
> dictated by the season
> manual
> tedious
> strain on body.

Wealthy: lots of leisure time to enjoy vast wealth.

Harsh existance
Poor living conditions for the majority:
> squalid housing
> poor hygiene
> bad health
> unvaried diet.

Only the upper class lived in luxury.

Communications
Poor: stayed in village. Would only travel to local market towns, if at all. Limited knowledge of outside world.

Wealthy: likely to have a house in London or another large city. Travelled by coach. Had an appreciation of urban and rural life.

Church
Had a strong influence on daily life. Various teachings limited leisure time and controlled behaviour – not always successfully!

Puritanism: teaching strong commitment to morality. Says 'man' is basically sinful and should have no idle time in which to be sinful.

Sabbatarianism: strict observance of the Sabbath[1] – i.e. no recreation on day of rest.

Evangelism: preached against gambling, drink, idleness.

1 Since the Reformation, the 'Sabbath' is usually applied to the 'Lord's Day' i.e. the first day of the week (Sunday) observed by Christians in commemoration of the resurrection of Christ. Hebrews consider the Sabbath (or Sabbat) to be the seventh day of the week (Saturday).

A summary of popular recreation

Local coding	games developed to suit the local community.	**Ritual**	often linked to Church or seasons.
Limited rules	who could write then down?	**Wagering**	the chance to win and escape from poverty (not approved by the Church).
Rural	the population lived in the countryside so the games were rural.	**Drink**	to escape from harsh reality.
Occasional	often linked to festivals which only happened a few times a year.	**Physical force**	rather than skill required.
		Players and spectators	often little distinction between the two groups.
Violent	e.g. mob football	**Group identity**	they could be part of a team.
Cruel	e.g. blood sports. An obvious link here with the harsh existence of villagers.	**Rowdy**	most in conflict with respectable society. Often damage done to property.

Public schools – introduction

> *Education for the more wealthy.*

The public (now = private) schools in Great Britain played a major part in the development and organization of games and sports in the 19th century. In fact, the foundation of most of the sports played today rest in the history of the British public school.

Types of public schools

The Clarendon Schools

> The nine exclusive schools of Eton, Harrow, Rugby, Shrewsbury, St Paul's, Westminster, Charter House, Merchant Taylors, Winchester.
> Initially set up for the children of upper-class families.
> Had been around for a long time

Examples:
Winchester founded in 1382, Eton in 1440), therefore had primitive facilities.

Proprietary colleges

> These were middle-class copies of the Clarendon schools. Were generally purpose built and well equipped. Attracted the children of wealthy industrialists.

Examples:
Cheltenham, Clifton, Marlborough, Malvern.

Endowed grammar schools

> These were free schools set up in most towns around the country. Their patron was the King or Queen who had endowed it. (Names like the King Edward IV Grammar School.)
> In the mid-19th century several became fee paying and were accepted as public schools.

Denominational schools

> These were linked to the Church.
> They were predominantly small until the late-19th century when some became accepted as public schools.

Popular recreation in public schools

Home

> Boys saw different sports played at home by their parents, family friends and the locals.

Royal Tennis
Field Sports (e.g. shooting and hunting)
Combat sports
Mob games
Bathing (swimming)

School

> These sports and games were brought in from home and tailored to suit each school. They were adapted to suit the facilities that the school had to offer (e.g. courtyards, quadrangles, long corridors, buttresses, open grassy areas). As a consequence of these differences there was a great variety between the schools. For example, football might be played in a courtyard or on grass. 'Eton fives' has an upper and a lower court and a buttress.

Boys

> The pupils had lots of free time so therefore engaged themselves in playing the games they invented.
> Mostly played by the senior boys. Juniors used to collect balls or provide a minor supporting role.
> Gambling and drinking surrounded the sports.

The game of rugby is said to have originated at Rugby School in 1823. While playing football, William Webb Ellis took it on himself to pick up the ball and run towards the opposition goal. Where do you think the oval-shaped ball originated?

Public schools – developing attitudes

> *The boys' sports become more organised.* Tom Brown's Schooldays *is meant to depict life in the public schools.*

The enlightened headmasters

Sports and games in the 18th and 19th centuries were not developed for what they were, but how they could influence pupils' behaviour at school. What could staff do to channel all that youthful energy, to toughen up the body, and to build character?

Support

Some headmasters realised that the boys had to do something constructive with their free time. They saw the sporting activities that the boys clearly enjoyed as a way of promoting a code of ethics that could instil the sort of attitude they wanted.

Schools

From the 1830s headmasters such as Dr Arnold of Rugby School, Mr Kennedy of Shrewsbury, and Mr Moberly of Winchester began to use sport for its educational values.

Rules

As a consequence of this support the games became more formal. **Rules** were written establishing relationships between players and basic playing **techniques**. Gradually, sport began to flourish and the House system expanded to include matches between teams from different Houses.

What could be gained from sport?

Most of the sport was still run by the boys, but staff began to appear on the sidelines to encourage their House teams. The heads hoped to take away the brutal discipline that was instilled by the senior boys and replace it with activities that were not anti-social. They wanted to encourage conformity to authority with acceptable guidelines.

The effect of the 'Blues'

In the final stage of the development of public school sport we see it becoming more organised.

University

The public school boys attend university and decide to develop their games. Gradually, they adjust the rules and begin to produce hybrid games that take the best aspects of the different sports.

The graduates

These filter out into society taking their sports with them. Some go back to the public schools and introduce their organised games.

Sport

> The young staff become involved in coaching and running sport.
> The schools employ professional coaches.
> The standard improves; facilities improve.
> Pattern of the school day changes: lessons in the morning, games in the afternoon.

Muscular Christianity

Here we see the development of a link between **manliness** and **godliness**. The Headmasters have recognised that games can prepare their boys for adult life.

Physical endeavour	Moral Integrity
> Health	> Social cohesion
> Activity	> Respect for authority
> Move from over-studying	> Development of leadership
> Toughen up an indulgent society	> Response to leadership

Tom Brown's Schooldays
by Thomas Hughes

Several extracts from this book, first published in 1857, can be used to highlight the code of ethics that the liberal headmasters hoped to establish by allowing the introduction of sport. In the book, the school is Rugby School, and the headmaster is Thomas Arnold (Head of Rugby School, 1828–42).

The rugby match

Tom, a new boy to the school, throws himself on the ball, thereby saving his house team from defeat. He is injured in the process. The Head of House picks him up, checks he is OK and congratulates Tom on his bravery.

Technical aspects
> Rules
> Pitch
> Teams
> Supporters
> Uniforms

Moral values
> Selflessness of Tom
> Putting team before self
> Looked after by Head of House
> Support from team members

The fight

Slogger Williams, a big boy, picks on Arthur. Tom steps in to stop the fight and ends up fighting against the bully. An epic fight takes place that is watched by the rest of the boys. It stops when the headmaster arrives. He questions the Head Boy about it. Later the Head Boy encourages Tom and Slogger to make it up.

Technical aspects
> Rules
> Supporters
> Seconds
> Ring formed by crowd

Moral values
> Tom stands up for the rights of Arthur
> Authority of Headmaster
> Forgiveness
> Authority of Head Boy

The cricket match

Tom, the captain of the team and playing his last match for the school, sends Arthur in to bat at a crucial stage of the match. He realises he may not win the game but sees it as a good learning experience for Arthur. After the game Tom has tea with his form master and discusses his time at Rugby School.

Technical aspects
> Rules
> Equipment
> Uniforms
> Tactics

Moral values
> Tom identifies the needs of Arthur over the need to win
> Relationship with staff
> Respect for rest of team over Tom's captaincy

Public schools – elitism and athleticism

> *What about women?*

Elite girls schools

Women in Victorian society were seen as inferior to men. They were valued in the home for looking after children and running the house. Education was not seen as important.

Ladies' academies

> In the early 18th century several ladies' academies were established. They were for the upper classes and varied a great deal in quality and cost. Some were more expensive than the most exclusive public schools.

> They taught dancing, a form of callisthenics, sewing, singing, playing the piano, verse speaking, posture and any other graces it was felt important for a woman to have.

Girls' schools

> By the mid-19th century there was an emergence of girls' private schools (e.g. Roedean in Sussex, Malvern College in Worcestershire, Cheltenham Ladies).

> The development of their sport was influenced by what the girls had seen at home, often played by their brothers.

> As these girls' schools developed after the boys, they developed more quickly. By the 1880s tennis and cricket were being played in girls' schools. The girls wore their normal clothing and the games did not involve contact.

> Gradually the 'medical' reasons for women not participating in sport were set aside.

The effects of public schools on the local community

How did having a public school education have an effect on the whole of society? Boys from the public schools went into all aspects of society – from the armed forces to medicine, to the Church, to teaching, to industry and to the legal system. This promoted and developed sport in all areas of the community.

Army

As the British Empire grew, sport was taken all over the world. All ranks of soldiers and sailors were encouraged to play.

Industry

The industrialists began to see the benefits of health and attitude that sport could have on their workforce. They gradually allowed their workers time to play and provided facilities.

Church

The values of the Church were seen to be upheld in sport. This officially approved sport for all classes. The church also developed its own teams for its parishioners.

The characteristics of public school athleticism

Development of education

Prior to mid-19th century

> Classical education – learning Latin and Greek.
> Leisure time of boys mis-spent – gambling, drinking, fighting.

By mid-19th century

> Wider social and intellectual education.
> Greater variety of subjects taught, relevant to the modern world.
> The whole person looked at.
> Pupils' leisure time becomes a time for games and sport.

Ethics

> Godliness and manliness.
> Social control – responsibility, respect, morality.
> Physical endeavour – moral integrity.

Facilities

> Sponsored by old boys.
> Purpose-built buildings.
> Playing fields.

Technical development of sport

> Regularity.
> Respectability.
> Codification.
> Well organised.

Muscular Christianity

> Win gracefully.
> Lose with honour.
> Bravery.
> Brotherhood.
> Leadership.

Changing attitudes of Heads

1 Heads actively discourage games – pupils flogged.
2 Then realise games promote values: some support given to House games; not actively discouraged.
3 Finally, Heads actively promote games/sports: allowed time; provided staff and facilities.

Rational recreation

> *We now see sport moving from the public schools into the community.*

How did sport become an activity for all?

How did team sports spread and develop across the length and breadth of the country?

How did the 'sport of kings' become a major spectator sport that all levels of society could enjoy?

We will try to answer these questions.

Mid-18th century social attitudes leading to the development of sport

Aristocracy

(upper class)

> Privileged elite
> Used to being in control
> Exclusive pastimes that only they could afford.

Middle class

> Made rich by the industrial revolution (from mid-18th c.)
> Had a social conscience
> Liked to look after the morality of the nation
> Large pressure to conform to their high moral ground.

Acceptance of sport

> Sport was gradually seen as an appropriate way of occupying the lower classes away from drinking and gambling, and other anti-social and morally low habits.
> Gradually more free time was granted allowing more opportunity for sport.

Physical changes leading to the development of sport

Let us start by looking at Britain in the 19th century. The industrial revolution is well under way.

Urbanization

The majority of the country's population now lived in the cities, rather than the countryside. This meant large concentrations of population needed meaningful leisure time activities to divert them from gambling and drinking.

Technology

Equipment – advances in materials led to better bats and balls. They lasted longer, were fairly regular in bounce and performance, and could be mass-produced.

Sports pitches – machines were invented to maintain and prepare pitches.

Timekeeping – stopwatches were developed allowing more accurate timekeeping.

Communications

Roads – improvement of road surfaces and the introduction of coach travel.

Rail – steam power meant the growth of the railway system.

These two developments allowed teams – and supporters – to move around the country to compete against each other.

Telegraph – this meant results and information could be sent quickly from one end of the country to another.

Printed word – the development of newspapers meant people could keep in touch with results of sports matches and sporting events.

Literacy – this was promoted. More people were able to take an interest in sports by reading newspapers and the like.

Working class

> Poor
> Uneducated
> Squalid living conditions
> Subservient

Living conditions

> Squalid
> Infant mortality high
> Poor sanitation
> Disease common

Working conditions

> Low wages
> Hazardous working environment – many accidents and deaths
> Long hours of work
  - prior to 1870, 72 hour week
  - after 1870, white collar workers had a half day off on Saturday
  - after 1880, the same was granted to most semi-skilled workers
  - after 1890, the rest were given a half day off each week.

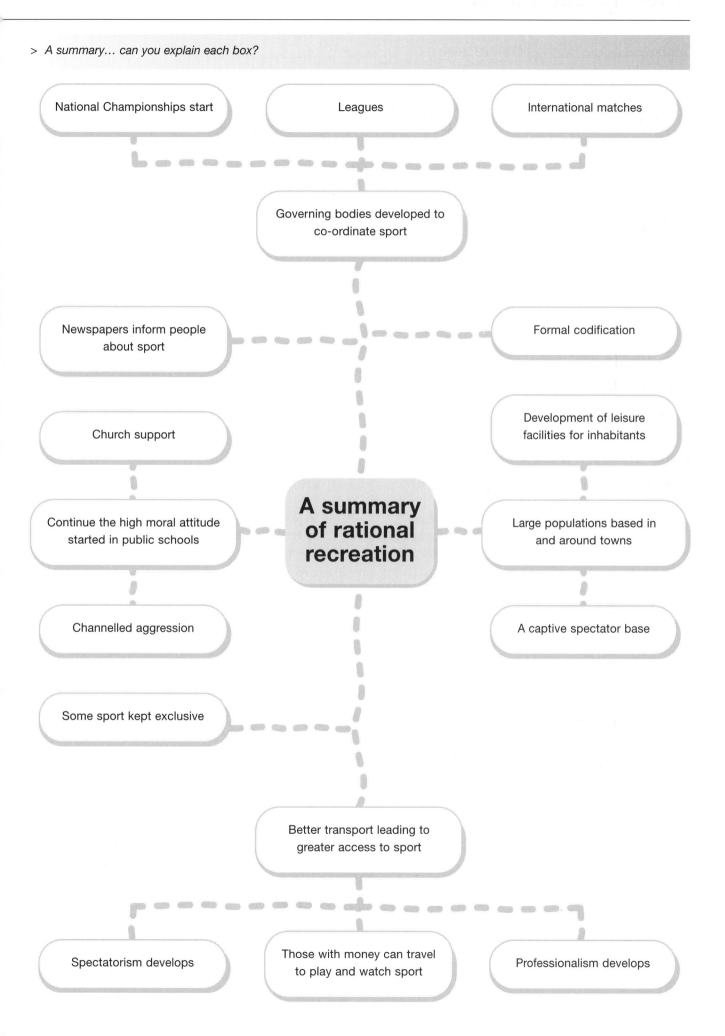

National Championships start

Leagues

International matches

Governing bodies developed to co-ordinate sport

Newspapers inform people about sport

Formal codification

Church support

Development of leisure facilities for inhabitants

A summary of rational recreation

Continue the high moral attitude started in public schools

Large populations based in and around towns

Channelled aggression

A captive spectator base

Some sport kept exclusive

Better transport leading to greater access to sport

Spectatorism develops

Those with money can travel to play and watch sport

Professionalism develops

> *Schooling before 1900 is minimal and varied.*

So what physical education was taught in state schools in the late 19th and early 20th centuries? 'Not a lot' may be the answer. For the lower classes in state schools, few pupils if any experienced games as their physical education consisted of structured physical training.

State physical education before 1902

Legislation

Before 1870

The education of those who could not afford a private education was the responsibility of the Church. The quality and accessibility of education varied a great deal. The majority remained uneducated.

The 1870 Forster Elementary Education Act

> This was the first step towards creating a **state education system**.

> It only made recommendations, however. As a consequence of this, improvement was not as complete as it could have been.

Mundella's Education Act, 1880

> This made it compulsory for all children between the ages of 5 and 10 to attend school.

> Led to a significant increase in the number of school places.

> By 1899 the school-leaving age had been raised to 12 years.

Facilities

The majority of schools that were in towns had little space for playing fields. There were those that also had no playground. This clearly placed restrictions on the sporting activities that could be offered.

Activities

> Prior to 1870 there was a mixture of Swedish, German and English gymnastics. Archibald Buchanan was the main proponent of the latter type of gymnastics. Once again there was a great deal of variety from school to school in content and regularity.

> In the 1870s Drill was developed, for boys and girls. This was taught by NCOs from the army.

> By the 1890s some of this drill was being taught by teachers.

Physical training 1902–1918

The Boer War (1899-1902)

> This war saw the British Army defeated by a band of men who were part-time soldiers. The health and fitness of the British troops was blamed, and it was felt that this was a consequence of inadequate physical training at school.

> Colonel Fox of the Army Physical Training Corps was appointed by the government to find a solution.

> Physical training remained part of the curriculum for the next fifty years.

1904 syllabus

> This identified two main areas: health and education.

> To achieve this, 109 exercise tables were drawn up. These were specific lesson plans that teachers or instructors could follow.

> It allowed for poor facilities, no equipment and the large numbers in classes.

> Three 20-minute lessons were to be held per week and, if possible, they should be outside.

1909 syllabus

> Over the year leading up to this syllabus more concern was taken over the welfare of children of working-class families.

> With this in mind, Dr Newman was appointed to the Board of Education. His influence ensured a slightly more therapeutic angle.

> The number of exercise tables was cut to 71 and some organised games were introduced. With these we see the first tentative move away from military-style PT teaching.

1902 model course

> The three main components of this course were:
>   – fitness
>   – familiarity with weapons
>   – discipline.

> It was to be delivered by military instructors.

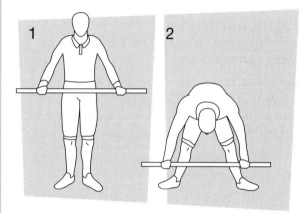

> The 1902 model course soon came under attack as it clearly did not take into account the educational aspect that should be the purpose of physical training in schools. It had children doing exercises designed for adults.

Commands

'Attention'   'Stand at ease'
'Head, turn'   'Trunk, turn'
'Marching on the spot'
'Marching, about turn'

Physical education in state schools – 1914/18–1988

> *Physical training shifts to become physical education.*

Physical training 1914–1939

The First World War

> The years 1914–1918 saw the tragedy of the first great world war. A generation of young men was almost totally wiped out. The effect this had on the education system is interesting.

> Firstly, it was recognised that a slightly more child-centred approach was needed. The authorities still wanted a disciplined and hard-working lower class, but they wanted them to show some initiative.

> Secondly, women had worked in munitions factories and on the land during the war. This increased their social status and afforded them more equality, as they had shown they could cope with demanding physical work.

1919 syllabus

> Dr Newman was once again involved with this.

> The syllabus allowed more freedom and individual interpretation in the use of the exercise tables.

> It also stated that during each session time should be set aside for games and dancing.

> For the older pupils therapeutic exercises were still the main emphasis.

1919–1932

This period in history was full of social upheaval. The biggest impact was from the economic depression that started in the late 1920s. This led to very poor living conditions for the less well off as they suffered even more than before. (There was no welfare state system so no unemployment benefit or family allowance.) The result was the production of the 1933 syllabus.

1933 syllabus

> This has been recognised as the best syllabus that the Board of Education in England and Wales had produced to date.

> It allowed more game play; introduced group work; but still kept some therapeutic aspects.

> At last we see a move from a teacher-centred approach to one where more choice is available and decisions can be made by pupils.

> Tables were still being produced to give teachers ideas, but they were less restrictive and more open to change.

Post Second World War physical education

The 1944 Butler Education Act

The emphasis here was on equal access to education for all, in theory.

The main points of it were:

1. Grammar schools were to be free, but selective. Pupils had to pass the 11+ exam to gain entry. Pupils from all economic backgrounds could now attend. (Those who did not pass the 11+ went to secondary modern schools.)
2. All children would leave primary school at 11, and start at the grammar or secondary modern school.
3. New schools were to be built to accommodate extra pupils.
4. The school-leaving age would be raised to 15.
5. Better forms of PE were to be devised for the older pupils.

The effect of the Second World War

> As with the First World War everyone was touched by the long, hard years of war. Due to the development of aircraft bombers and long-range missiles, the lives of everyone in Britain, including children, were affected directly. People looked to their children for hope and we now see a further step towards child-centred learning.

> The training that had been used to create 'thinking' soldiers during the war was now adapted to suit schools. Assault course type equipment was put up in schools – ropes, benches, ladders and climbing frames. Pupils were required to use their initiative and take responsibility for each other.

> Leading educationalists introduced 'modern' dance and gymnastics. The latter could also require equipment.

> Variety and enjoyment, as well as high levels of skill learning now became important. This led to the publication of two documents by the ministry of Education: *Moving and Growing* (published in 1952) and *Planning the Programme* (1953).

Education Reform Act, 1988

Reinforced the position of PE in British schools, making it a compulsory subject. However, it was only in 1992 that the government decided the details of the bill. Revised in 1995 following the publication of the Dearing Report in state education.

National Curriculum

This provides that pupils in schools should have similar experiences in PE irrespective of where they live in the country. Applies to all state schools.

Pupils in different school years allocated to **key stages** (see table). The PE programme in every school will have similarities. However, every school has different facilities and equipment will vary, so there will be variations in PE up and down the country.

Key Stage	Pupil's age	Year group	Activities in PE
1	5–7 years	1–2	Games, gymnastic activities, dance
2	7–11 years	3–6	Games, gymnastic activities, dance, athletic activities, outdoor and adventurous activities, swimming. Pupils to be taught the six areas of activity
3	11–14 years	7–9	Pupils taught four of the above activities
4	14–16 years	10–11	Pupils taught a minimum of two of above activities. One must be a game

Physical education and sport

> *Sports are at the core of physical education.*

Physical education and sport

At the heart of all physical education are sporting activities. PE is a school subject.

In PE and in sport participants learn:

> how to perform in sports, e.g. swimming strokes, dribbling in hockey, ball control in soccer.

> through taking part in physical activity.

Extra-curricular activities

> These are games and sports that take place outside normal school time.

> For most children, physical education at school is their first contact with organised sport. (Although they may have learned to swim before starting school.)

> At school, children have the opportunity not only to take part in a range of physical activities during lessons, but also in organised games during lunchtime, after school and against other schools.

Interschool competition

This is considered important in developing high standards of play. However, the activities involved depend on a number of factors:

> Which activities are included in the school PE curriculum.

> Facilities available to the school.

> Interests and skills of the staff.

> Coaches and parents might be involved in PE, school teams and organised matches.

Differences between teaching PE and coaching a sport

PE teaching	Sports coaching
> time is spent on general exercise	> more time is spent on an activity
> participants are there because it is part of the curriculum	> the participants are usually there by choice
> groups are of mixed ability	> groups being coached are often of a similar ability
> the social aspect is as important as the skill acquisition	> selective

Summary

Which of the following words could be linked to the dates listed below?

1902	1909	1919	1933	1944

Teaching style	Facilities	Equipment	Educational values
Command	Classroom	Batons	Accepting authority
Discovery	Playground	Poles	Subject centred
Problem solving	Gymnasium	Ropes	Child centred
Authoritarian	Playing field	Benches	Physical skills
Formal		Climbing frames	Social skills
Informal		Boxes	Therapeutic
Progressive			
Traditional			

Games and activities

> *Sport has now become far more organised.*

Many activities and games were developed in the latter half of the 19th century and the early years of the 20th century. Below are a few which highlight the level and speed of development.

Football

This was popular with all sections of society. It is a game that began with the lower classes and was refined in the public schools.

Notable dates:

1863: Some school old boys' teams founded the Football Association (FA)

1885: Professionalism was made legal

1888: The Football League was started.

By the early 1900s there were 10000 clubs within the FA

Athletics

Athletics was initially developed in the public schools. It was copied from the ancient Greeks.

We can also see an influence from the early days of pedestrianism where the wealthy would arrange races between their footmen (servants).

Notable dates:

1860s: Gradual appearance of athletics meetings; founding of Thames Hare and Hounds cross-country club

1866: Amateur Athletics Club formed

1880: Amateur Athletics Association (AAA) born

1913: International Amateur Athletics Federation (IAAF) founded

Swimming

Public baths – these were cheap and consequently used by poorer citizens. They promoted exercise and hygiene.

Turkish baths – these were more exclusive and from these we see the development of competitive swimming. Competition swimming became popular, particularly in London, in the 19th century.

Notable dates:

1869: First organised swimming governing body (London)

1874: First national swimming championships

1884: Formation of the Amateur Swimming Association (ASA)

1905: Fédération Internationale de Natation Amateur (FINA) – world governing body – founded in London

1926: First European championship

Tennis

Lawn tennis evolved slowly. It developed from handball, an outdoor game popular in France.

This was a game for the middle classes. It was developed as a cheaper form of sport than 'real tennis'. It could be played in the garden at home but also clubs sprang up that the middle classes could join.

Cricket

This was a game participated in by all sections of society. The fact that it was non-contact and it promoted gentlemanly behaviour contributed to this.

In the late 19th century we see the development of cricket grounds as the middle class begin to support games.

Notable dates:

1864: First county championship

1873: Qualification of the sport's rules for county cricketers

1875: Modern rules drawn up by the Marylebone Cricket Club (MCC)

1877: 1 March – first 'Test' match in Melbourne, Australia

1880: Kennington Oval staged first Test match in England

Notable dates:

1871: First lawn tennis club in the world formed at Manor House Hotel, Leamington Spa

1873: First book of rules. Major Clopton Wingfield patented a 'new and improved court for playing the ancient game of tennis' – shaped like an hourglass

1876: The All-England Croquet and Lawn Tennis Club established at Wimbledon

Historical issues – amateur *v* professional

> *Sport as an occupation or preoccupation.*

Throughout the history of sport there have been debates over what is the difference between an 'amateur' and a 'professional' in sport. In recent years there has been a growth in the number of professional sportsmen and women. Think of sports such as athletics and rugby union. Basically, there are three types of sportsperson:

> Amateurs – who take part in sport for enjoyment and do not get paid or receive prize money.

> Professionals – who are paid (some highly!) to take part in sport – playing, coaching or managing. For these people sport is their job.

> Semi-professionals – who are paid for playing, coaching or managing but also have another job. For these people, sport alone does not pay enough.

A brief history of amateur *v* professional

In the Ancient Greek Olympics athletes only received a laurel wreath for winning. There was no prize money. However, to be good enough to win, these athletes had to be able to train, eat the right food, and use the best equipment (javelins, discuses, etc.). Their normal work (usually as soldiers) would not have paid for all this. Instead they were supported by wealthy individuals, or given help by their employers. Although these athletes were amateur, they did receive some financial support.

18th and 19th centuries

The gentleman amateur
He was wealthy so could take time off to play sport. The 'gentleman amateur' competed to prove himself as a person and to test his ability. He did not train as that would make him a 'professional'. He was a respected member of the community with a good education.

The professional
He was generally from a poor background, therefore had to make money from sport. If he could not make money then he could not afford to play. The professional was perceived to be corruptible as he was controlled by money (i.e. might take a bribe to throw a game or contest).

The middle class
They could not afford time off work to play sport, but at the same time did not want to get paid to play. They admired the high cultural values of the gentleman amateur. They played in their free time.

Early professionals

1. The **prize fighter** was paid to represent the noble. All sections of society watched and wagered.
2. **Wager boats** – the river men would race each other. Spectators would place bets on the fastest crossings.
3. **Footmen** – the wealthy would match their footmen (servants) and place bets on the winners. This was the start of pedestrianism (professional running).
4. **Cricket** was one of the first truly professional games. Between 1750 and 1850 there were several professional touring teams taking part in matches in all parts of the country. Cricket coaches were employed at the large country houses to prepare wickets, coach the owners and to play for their teams. Later they worked in public schools (see page 105).

Developments

> The modern Olympic Games began in 1896, with the intention that amateurs would compete against one another. There would be no prize money for the winners, only medals.

> As sports developed there was more scope for professionalism. To be a good player you needed to devote time and money to training. You needed money to attract the best players to your team in order that you could do well in the leagues and attract supporters.

> As the class system gradually eroded, the stigmatism of being a professional diminished.

> The abolition of the maximum wage meant players could negotiate wages and turn from tradesmen into professionals.

> In soccer the maximum wage in England was £4 in 1900. George Eastham, of Newcastle United, went on strike in 1961 over the maximum wage (£10 then). A couple of years later, Johnny Haynes of Fulham became the first £100-a-week soccer player.

Historical issues – women and sport

> Historically, women's opportunity in sport has been far less than men's.

The Victorian era (1837–1901)

> This era had the biggest single effect on limiting women's participation in sport.

> It was felt during this time that women should not exert themselves physically as it was not good for their health and it was not 'ladylike'. Dress had to completely cover their body, thus limiting their ability to move freely. Things remained like this until after the First World War (1914–1918).

> The daughters of wealthy families who received an education did so at a ladies academy, or one of the new private schools. The former concentrated on social graces. The latter gradually broadened its outlook and allowed some 'ladylike' sports (such as tennis and hockey).

> Working-class women were almost totally excluded from sport. Their only experience was in the late 1800s – with drill (see page 113).

Madame Bergman-Osterbeg

> This lady was involved with PE in London and among other achievements introduced a ladies PE College in 1895. This influenced the spread of women's sport.

> Some of her former pupils set up their own colleges, thereby encouraging more female PE teachers to enter the profession.

> Madame Bergman-Osterberg's philosophy was based around a mixture of Swedish gymnastics and team games. She advocated single sex lessons.

Female sports

Field sports – these were participated in by the upper class and were on the privacy of their own land. Women joined in with these social occasions.

Archery – this was non-contact and used no physical exertion.

Garden games – tennis, croquet and badminton were all adopted by the middle classes. They could be played at home in the privacy of their garden.

Golf – clubs allowed women to play at certain off-peak times. They were discriminated against.

Athletics – the women's AAA, formed in 1922, promoted athletics. The 1928 Olympics were the first games in which women were allowed to compete. The fact that several competitors were ill after the 800-metre race caused a real setback – a case of 'I told you so'!

Restricted opportunity

Even today there are less opportunities available for women.

> They cannot compete in as many events in the Olympics as men, and in professional sports they generally get paid less.

> The media focuses on them less.

The Women's Sports Federation (WSF)

This association was founded in 1984 to help women become more involved in sport at all levels. You can find out more about WSF from their website: www.wsf.org.uk

USA (1)

> *Cultural factors which influence sport in America.*

We will begin our comparative studies by looking at games and sport – and the wider curriculum – in North America. The focus is on the United States of America (USA). In many ways the USA is a world leader: the way that sportsmen and women are treated, the facilities available, and the way major sports are funded.

History

> Native American Indians played lacrosse as Baggatoway.

> Many Native American Indians were killed by Europeans who settled on the East Coast (//[1] Australian Aborigines).

> Colonialists were pioneers migrating west. 'Frontier spirit' developed – the spirit of survival in alien territory, a sense of adventure.

> Sports reflected the origin of the colonialists in areas where they settled – hunting, horseracing, cricket, rugby: middle-class English.

> Many sports suffered from the imported Puritanism. [Many early English and Dutch settlers were Puritans, who lived according to strict moral and religious principles. They avoided physical activities such as sport.]

> The War of Independence (1863–6) severed the links with their European past and sport reflected the emergence of an American identity:
  – from rugby came 'gridiron' (American football)
  – rowing and athletics – intercollegiate competitions
  – baseball established 1860
  – volleyball developed some time after as a pastime for exercise-seeking businessmen
  – James Naismith invented basketball in 1891 as a game to be played indoors in winter, while attending a YMCA (Young Men's Christian Association) training School.
  – Middle-class women played tennis and croquet, and cycled.

Ideology

> The '**American Dream**' – 'rags to riches'. The idea that everyone and anyone can achieve success/the pursuit of happiness. Sport is seen as a way out of the gutter (e.g. boxing).

> **Win ethic** – winning is the only thing. This is also known as the Lombardian philosophy, after Vince Lombardi, Head Coach of Green Bay Packers in 1959, who transformed them from a losing American Football team into a major power in the sport. The emphasis is on competition and rewards. Professionalism and commercialism – society only interested in winners.

> **Radical ethic** – winning is important but so also is the process – intrinsic value (the middle way).

> **Counter-culture ethic** – some Americans are trying to change the focus and suggest that it is not whether you win or lose but 'how you play the game'.

Political

> Decentralised

> Federal republic, with elected president

> 2 elected Houses – Senate and Congress

> Two-party system – Democrats and Republicans

> 51 states (// Australia) almost independent; each has own parliament and funding

> A young society 'looking for identity and forming a modern unified nation, forging their way with their 'frontier spirit'.

---

1 Symbol denotes 'parallel'. These draw out comparisons with the other comparative studies in this section.

Geography

Population: 250 million

¾ live in cities, therefore population dense in cities and sparse in other areas.

Climate: Every kind – from very cold (High Plains) to semitropical (Gulf Coast), rainy (Central Plain + Appalachians) and desert (// Australia).

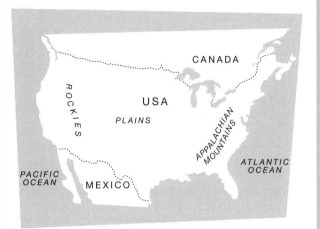

Size: 3.5 million square miles

(// Australia but population 15 times as large)

51 states: Alabama, Alaska, Arizona, Arkansas, California, Colorado, Connecticut, Delaware, District of Columbia, Florida, Georgia, Hawaii, Idaho, Illinois, Indiana, Iowa, Kansas, Kentucky, Louisiana, Maine, Maryland, Massachusetts, Michigan, Minnesota, Mississippi, Missouri, Montana, Nebraska, Nevada, New Hampshire, New Jersey, New Mexico, New York, North Carolina, North Dakota, Ohio, Oklahoma, Oregon, Pennsylvania, Rhode Island, South Carolina, South Dakota, Tennessee, Texas, Utah, Vermont, Virginia, Washington, West Virginia, Wisconsin, Wyoming.

> Each state is approximately equivalent to a European country but with less population.

3 geographical areas which are very varied:

1. highland (Appalachians to the East)
2. plains (central America)
3. mountains (Rockies to the West)

Still many wilderness areas (// Australia).

Communications

> Airlines and interstate buses (called 'greyhounds') are heavily used.
> Transcontinental railways.
> Heavy car usage – long distances to travel.

Social/economic

> A capitalist society, where commercialism is strong; based on private enterprise.
> Material wealth is important.
> Individuals tend to identify with their state rather than nation. People are New Yorkers or Californian first; American second. Sport is a way to nationalism with the flag, oath and national anthem to remind them.
> ¾ population white; ¼ black. Last into the country tend to be at the bottom of the social ladder.
> Stacking

WASPS

Black community

Puerto Ricans

Mexicans

Vietnamese

WASPS – White Anglo-Saxon Protestants (privileged and affluent)

> Many racial groups. Society does not let them move up the ladder to a position of power – 'glass ceiling'.
> Racial groups identify with specific sports (e.g. basketball 'dream team' had few whites; certain nationalities play particular positions in gridiron).
> Pluralist society – the right of every ethnic group to keep its identity.

Excellence

Win ethic

> Striving for excellence is developed through interscholastic and intercollegiate sport and sports scholarships.
> Few sports schools because all schools aim to achieve excellence. School sport generates its own funding – very big occasion covered by the media.
> Draft system – football and basketball clubs have choice of college students who are 'drafted' to professional teams.
> Commercial enterprise of collegiate football and basketball funds scholarships. Federal money is used to finance the Olympic team. Motivated to win by need to beat other superpowers.

USA (2)

> *Thematic considerations of sport in the USA. Compare these with other countries.*

Education, PE + sport

> Predominantly free state education, plus some private schools linked to Church groups. Each state is responsible for education (states vary considerably with climate and geography, so education more relevant to own state).

> Administered by local District School Board (DSB). Policy is <u>not</u> devolved to individual schools. Kindergarten (4–5); elementary (6–12), high school (12–17). The aim of all is to pass high-school diploma.

> Physical Education is part of the curriculum – work on the physical, mental, social and emotional development of the child. High schools have fitness testing. This suits the culture – the importance of being the best, and accountability.

> Sports are more important than PE in the USA. Therefore the PE teacher has lower status and is separate from the sports coach (although they are trying to improve the importance of PE).

> Counter-culture – heuristic[1] approach conflicts with competitive ethic.

> Inter-scholastic sport is very important. Schools often have excellent facilities and are self-supporting (charging for entrance to matches etc.). It can be elitist – everything is spent on the most able. Coaches are highly paid but are expected to produce results ('hire and fire').

> Legislation to bring equality of programme and funding to boys and girls – female performer in professional sport was the cheerleader!

> Adaptive programme for children with special needs.

> Intercollegiate sport – Harvard and Yale reflected the traditions of Oxford and Cambridge but abandoned the amateurism. 2 divisions:
> 1. National Association of Inter-collegiate Athletics (NAIA) responsible for the control of athletic competitions between smaller colleges.
> 2. National Collegiate Athletic Association (NCAA) responsible for inter-scholastic programme at larger colleges.

> Individual sports governing bodies replaced Amateur Athletic Union (AAU).

> Sports scholarships to universities – sport is seen by coaches to be more important than academic studies - increases pressure on students.

> Sport is entertainment and commercial – big business.

Mass participation

> No specific plans by the federal government.

> Programmes for adults are part of school programmes.

> For children, 'little league sport' (e.g. little league basketball) – originally set up by parents, now a business organisation catering for 8–18 year olds (senior division 13–15; big league 16–18). Attracts media coverage.

> National senior sports organisation - image of a healthy old age.

> No real private sports clubs except elitist ones (tennis and golf). Expensive. Less wealthy involved with activities at:
> – ice rinks
> – swimming pools
> – basketball courts.

> All interested in going to the game (baseball).

Outdoor education/ outdoor recreation

> Outdoor education is a tradition in USA but it is out of school. Children go every year to summer camp (// France). Programmes introduce Americans to nature but socialisation is important too. Some are privately run, others by organisations such as the YMCA.

> Pioneer/frontier spirit – to overcome alien environment. The variety of landscape gives scope for challenging and exciting experiences.

> National parks are under federal law. State parks administered by state.

> Many go to enjoy these wilderness areas. Land is classified according to isolation:
> 1 – close to towns; 5 – wilderness

Safety is important particularly with risky sports becoming more popular and the dangers in the wilderness areas.

---

1 Methods of learning which involve reasoning and part experience rather than solutions that are given to you by a teacher/coach.

France (1)

> *Cultural factors which influence sport in France.*

We now turn our attention to the European continent. With so many countries to choose from, it would not be possible to cover all adequately. Instead we will focus on France.

History

France is bordered by many countries (see map); French people have lived under the constant threat of invasion.

> Involved in many wars on the European mainland.
> – French Revolution (1789–94) – aristocracy overthrown. *Liberté, Equalité et Fraternité* – resulted in closed frontiers and closed minds to outsiders.
> – Napoleonic Wars (1836–40)
> – two world wars (1914–18 and 1939–45).

> History has influenced sport in France:
> – initially associated with upper classes (aristocracy) and the Court of Louis XIV
> – high culture – fencing, tennis
> – post French Revolution, sport became militarised during Napoleonic Wars – physical training, gymnastics.

> French Empire is spread over 4 continents.

> 19th century: middle-class sport influenced by **Baron de Coubertin** – amateurism – established the modern Olympic Games in 1896.

> Old colonial power with strong traditions developed a more liberal colonial policy than Britain.

> **Assimilation** of colonial natives who were granted French citizenship (Algerian, Moroccan). France calls on them for selection to its national teams.

Geography

Population: 56 million, of whom 1/5 live in Paris. Concentration of wealth and power is in the capital city.

Much of land area bordered by sea.

Many rivers.

Convenient for Alps and Pyrenees (skiing; mountain climbing).

Climate: Varied, different in the North and South
> Maritime
> Mediterranean
> Alpine

Supports a wide range of sports and recreational activities.

Size: 200000 square miles (cf. UK: 94000 square miles)

Paris is centre of administration and finance. It also has the major tourist attractions.

Communications:
> All roads and railways radiate from Paris.
> Routes National and motorways.
> Approximately same population as UK, but twice the size.

Because the geography is varied, with different climates, it allows for lots of water sports – sailing, swimming, fishing – as well as skiing, climbing and cycling.

France (2)

> *Thematic considerations of sport in France. Compare with other countries.*

Ideology

Nationalism

> In the post-war period President de Gaulle reinforced a feeling of nationalism.

> 'Every Frenchman is born a soldier' – feeling of being French is important.

> Rural simplicity and 'taste' – whether it be food, wine or theatre.

> Retention of their language (keen to eliminate English words).

> Intellect important – academic study is a priority (therefore PE is poorly rated in schools).

> Baccalaureate system in upper schools.

> The French enjoy a spectacle (e.g. Tour de France).

> They let themselves go and appreciate the diversity of the countryside.

> They love a test of manliness.

> In sport, play with flair (e.g. World Cup soccer and rugby).

> The French consider the way you win is as important as winning (Olympianism).

Political

Democratic system

France has been a republic (since the Revolution).

> Elected president

> Many political parties

> Government – centralised control, reflected in organisation of sport, recreation and PE.

> Secretary of State for Youth and Sport (*de la Jeunesse et de Sport*) appointed (// UK Minister of Sport).

> Provision made for sport as part of a central policy.

> Participate in international events – rugby, football – but have own established event (Tour de France).

Social/economic

Stacking

Aristocratic families and Parisienne[1]

Algerians and other immigrants

> Capitalist economy – with Paris as the economic capital.

> Split into provinces. In a market economy sport is important because it raises money through sponsorship.

> Different ethnic groups have own language and maintain own spirit and pastimes; own identity e.g. French Basque, Bretons, Catalans (// UK – England, Scotland, Ireland, Wales).

> Immigrants from French colonies – Algerian, Moroccan. Live very much within their own boundaries and try to establish own culture.

> Sports – pelota, bullfighting, boule, petanque (// UK – Highland Games).

> Sports are rurally and agriculturally based. Very proud of them locally.

> August is national holiday month (5 weeks) – leave to go to the coast.

1 Parisienne – super elite bourgeoise middle class.

Mass participation

> *'Sport pour tous'* campaign to promote sport for all (// UK).

> Aim to convince the public of the necessity to participate in physical activities. Specifically aimed at non-participating adults. As members of sports clubs people are registered and have a licence, the government is able to monitor the level of participation.

> The French are encouraged to be active for pleasure and health.

Education, PE and sport

> Strong intellectual tradition. State schools – provide free tuition at all secondary schools (// comprehensive system in UK).
> Few private schools (Catholic).
> State-controlled centralised education policy but the further from Paris, less influence the policy appears to have.
> Primary (6–10); secondary (11–18 years); baccalaureate exam at 18.
> Physical education is under the control of the Secretary of State for Youth and Sport.

Primary

Concentrate on physical and psychological development.

Le Tiers Temps Pedagogique (of 27 hours a week at school, 6 hours should be spent on PE (*le gym*) and sport.

Secondary

Compulsory PE and sport sessions delivering *'Le Program'* – syllabus for teachers.

'Le gym' PE is formally assessed with practical tests at:

15– *Brevet de Colleges*
17– *Brevet d'Enseignement Professionel*
18– Baccalaureate (// Australia)

> Sport is more important than PE. Sport within the school – sports associations provide competitive educational events. PE teachers are involved. (Tends to be conflict between clubs and schools.)

1. *Union Nationale de Sport Scolaire* (UNSS – runs sport outside schools). Separated from ASSU (*L'Association de Sport Scolaire et Universités*) in 1975.

2. FNSU (university sport).

UNSS

> Sporting activities are taught out of school at local sport centres (*Centres d'Animation Sportive – CAS*).
> Voluntary – only a small percentage of pupils attend.
> Not taught by teachers unless they choose to.
> Runs numerous competitions.
> Sport is either Olympic or non-Olympic.

EUREPS

> Teacher training – PE teachers are trained at *Unites d'Education de Reserche de l'Education Physique et Sport*.
> Special units attached to universities. Took over from ENSEP.

Outdoor education/ outdoor recreation

> *Les Classes Transplantées* – part of curriculum – classes in outdoor education. Children taken to the country to appreciate the natural environment and regions of France. Develop outdoor pursuit skills as well as having normal lessons:
  Classes de mer (sea/sailing)
  Classes de neige (mountain snow/skiing)
  Classes de vert (countryside)
> *Colonie de vacance* aimed at disadvantaged groups. Gives inner-city children the opportunity to visit the countryside etc. Some run privately (// US summer camps). Parents take separate holidays from children who have camp experience.
> *Le Plein Air* – love of fresh air. Enjoy being out and seeing nature.

Excellence

> Following poor results at the 1960 Rome Olympics, which hurt their national pride, President Charles de Gaulle wanted sporting success. He addressed the organisation and funding of sport with his 5-point plan.
> State aid was given to improve facilities in most French towns, and given administrative support.
> In 1970, INSEP (National institute of PE and sport) was created from merging INS (National sports institute) and ENSEPS (teacher training establishment). This was a centre for excellence which had a sports study section for children.

Talent identification

> Talent identification starts with the Brevet d'Aptitude Physique (8–12 year olds).
> Regional sport study section (11–29 year olds)
> INSEP has special sections within schools. The talented are selected to attend – must not interfere with academic study.
> Schools specialise in certain sports – excellent facilities and coaching.
> Sports divided into Olympic and non-Olympic.

Australia (1)

> *Cultural factors which influence Australian sport.*

As a final comparative study, we will look at Australasia, with particular reference to Australia.

History

> Aboriginal culture – went through cycle of oppression. Aborigines (native Australians) seen by European settlers as sub-human and were presumed dangerous (// Native American Indians).

> When settlers wanted their territory, the Aborigines were forced inland so that the European arrivals could settle by the coast. The colonialists moved in and suggested 'white' was better.

> Missionaries and soldiers tried to destroy the Aboriginal culture.

> Australia became a British colony – the colonies becoming self-governing.

> At the end of 19th century – the Commonwealth of Australia was formed.

> Sport reflects the developments in the UK – predominantly middle class as little industrialism.

> Colonial influence was considerable and can be seen in the sports played (e.g. rugby and cricket). They still like to beat the 'old enemy' (England).

> Later took in other Europeans, South Africans and Asians.

Ideology

> 'Sun, sea and surf' (// USA; France).

> It is suggested that sport is an obsession to Aussies. Certainly the 'win ethic' is strong (// USA).

> Because of colonial influence, they adopted many of the British/Celtic ethics.

> Strong sense of survival in alien environment.

> Aboriginals at home in the natural environment.

> 'Dream time' – go walkabout to find self in nature.

> They are trying to re-establish the Aboriginal culture by claiming back land through the courts. They re-enact their culture for the tourists (// North American Indians).

Political

The 5 states all have a federal democracy.

Political parties – National Party, Labour Party, Liberal Party – mix of British and USA systems.

> Pre 1950 – predominantly British/Irish descent and some displaced Europeans.

> Post-war – there was a need (1950s) to repopulate. Encouraged British to go, then took in other Europeans e.g. Greeks, Italians, Germans.

> 1960s – middle eastern and north African immigrants.

> 1970s – Asians admitted (affected business).

> 1990s – achieved quota for new settlers – now control numbers of immigrants.

Therefore Australia is a diverse multi-cultural society, but there is a limit to the population it can support.

Social/economic

> A prosperous capitalist country based on agriculture but developing new technology (Asian influence). Rich material wealth but high unemployment.

> Young society (// USA).

> Pluralist society quickly developed (// USA).

> Pluralism – every ethnic group has a right to their own identity (// USA).

> Assimilation – ethnic groups mixed in. Acceptable if done freely (France and UK); not acceptable if done by force.

> Separatism – works if both groups are equal but the more powerful can often try to remove weak – to be discouraged.

Anglo-Celt

Greeks and Italians

South-East Asians

Geography

Population: Approximately 18 million

> Population density is very low. Mostly live in major cities (80% of population is urban) in the coastal areas.

> 34% of Australia is desert which is mostly unpopulated and uninhabitable – Red Centre – alien territory.

> Great Divide – mountain range to East, running north to south.

> Tourists tend to go into the Bush; Aussies stay at home and watch sport.

> Climate – southern hemisphere (North – tropical; South – temperate). Allows for seasonal sports to be played all year (e.g. skiing). Healthy outdoor philosophy (can ski and surf in same day).

Size: Almost as big as the whole of Europe or North America.

6 states:

Western Australia (capital: Perth)

Victoria (capital: Melbourne)

Queensland (capital: Brisbane)

New South Wales (capital: Sydney)

Northern Territory (capital: Darwin)

Tasmania (capital: Hobart)

Communications: Good roads along coast and between major cities. 'Red Centre' mostly dirt tracks. Good rail and internal air services.

Mass participation

> **Aussie sport**

Programme to develop young people through sport – focus on juniors. Included are codes of behaviour. Programmes included Sportstart, Sportit and CAPS.

> **Active Australia**

To encourage participation of whole population (6–60). Achieved the need to expand the base of pyramid, which leads to 'excellence'.

Sports

> Adopted colonial sports – cricket, rugby union, horse racing.

> From immigrants – football.

> Established own sporting identity – swimming; Aussie rules.

Aussie rules

This sport developed in 1840s, as a mixture of rugby and Gaelic football. Played mainly in 4 states but with great intensity. A 40-a-side game of Aussie rules played in Melbourne in 1858 was abandoned – after 3 weeks.

Australia (2)

> *Thematic considerations of sport in Australia. Compare with other countries.*

Excellence

Have a desire to do well in Olympics, Commonwealth Games and cricket Test matches.

Poor performances in the 1976 Olympics led to change (// France).

> ASC (Australian Sports Commission) researched in other countries to look for the most effective method to select and train athletes. Set up the AIS (Australian Institute of Sport), an academy of sport in Canberra (where the federal government and ASC are located). Realised need for more than one institute of excellence.

> Set up more in other states – Queensland (at Brisbane); Western Australia (at Perth); South Australia (at Adelaide); Victoria (at Melbourne); New South Wales (at Sydney) – each specialised in one sport (e.g. cricket at Adelaide; rugby at Brisbane).

> Now each state devolved with centres of excellence in their main city. All part of the AIS federal system. Have programme of talent identification – Sportsleap, Sports search – run at all levels (to identify talent).

> Aussie able – provision for disabled athletes – some sports schools.

Outdoor education and outdoor recreation

> Within schools there is a programme of outdoor education that students can elect to study (not compulsory; // UK). The emphasis is on knowing about the importance of safety, conservation and recreation – *education in the outdoors*. A positive physical experience in the natural environment.

> Outward bound centres, e.g. Timbertops (// Gordonstoun in UK). There is a tendency to think of Australians as outdoor people but most live in cities.

> Outdoor recreation is associated with the beach as large cities tend to be near the coast. Therefore good water sports – yachting, windsurfing, rowing. The rest of Australia is pretty hostile.

> DASETT (Department of the Arts, the Environment, Tourism and Territories) has administrative control over the large areas of wilderness and deserts. Specific codes of behaviour.

> National parks are controlled by the local state, except for the Great Barrier Reef (popular for tourism).

Education, PE + sport

> Education is compulsory 6–15 years. Comprehensive (// USA; UK). Colonialist roots.

> Free, although fee-paying schools associated with religious bodies (// France).

> 'School of the air' is a system whereby programmes are transmitted by radio and television to outlying stations. Students receive tuition over the airwaves.

> Some funding allocated by federal government from taxes, but each state has the responsibility for education within the state (// USA).

Administered by:

DSE (Department of School Education)

Responsible for educational context of syllabus, sport and teacher training. Much has now been passed onto individual schools (// UK). PE or PASE (Physical and Sports Education) is compulsory throughout school years, but optional in Year 12 where can be taken as part of HSC (Higher School Certificate) [// A level PE in UK; Baccalaureate in France].

ACHPER (Australian Council for Health, Physical Education and Recreation)

Provides federal input, is committed to programmes and projects both commercial and educational. Its mission is to promote healthy lifestyles for all Australians. Has physical education development programme.

Questions

> The questions here are examples of the style of question that occur in the final papers.
> The information to answer these questions can be found in the relevant sections of this book.
> *(For answers and guidance, see pages 133-9)*

Applied anatomy and physiology

1 Explain, how the Sliding Filament theory applies to muscular contraction. *(5 marks)*

2 Describe the characteristics of fast twitch and slow twitch fibres; relate the differences in function to the differences in structure. *(7 marks)*

3 (a) Describe the structure of a motor unit. *(2 marks)*

(b) Explain why not all muscle fibre in a particular muscle contract at the same time. *(2 marks)*

(c) How does the human body increase the size of the force of muscle contraction? *(4 marks)*

4 (a) Describe what happens to a student's heart rate during a lesson in which he or she completes a bleep test. *(5 marks)*

(b) Draw a graph to represent this. *(7 marks)*

5 What is the relationship between heart rate and stroke volume with respect to cardiac output? *(3 marks)*

6 How does training effect the values of these parameters? *(3 marks)*

7 Explain the electrical conduction system of the heart. *(6 marks)*

8 Explain the 'lub' and the 'dub' heart sound heard through a stethoscope during the cardiac cycle. *(4 marks)*

9 Explain how the heart rate is controlled by the medulla oblongata. *(5 marks)*

10 (a) Describe the structural difference between an artery and a vein. *(3 marks)*

(b) Link the differences in structure to the function of each vessel. *(5 marks)*

11 Define the following: 'minute volume', 'tidal volume' and 'respiratory rate'. *(3 marks)*

12 Explain how an athlete would use knowledge of the centre of gravity to help achieve a more efficient sprint start. *(3 marks)*

13 How would knowledge of the effect of lever help a golfer improve their game? *(3 marks)*

Acquisition of skills

14 What is ability? Give three examples of abilities. *(5 marks)*

15 Using an example from sport, explain the open loop theory of motor control. *(5 marks)*

16 Using the example of catching a cricket ball, explain the closed loop theory of motor control. *(5 marks)*

17 Feedback can do many things for a performer.

(a) How does feedback affect the motivation of a beginner? *(2 marks)*

(b) How might you change the type of feedback for a more experienced performer? *(2 marks)*

18 Explain, with practical examples, reaction time, movement time and response time. *(3 marks)*

19 There are believed to be three stages or phases of learning; name them. *(3 marks)*

20 Explain the benefits of using a distributed practice style with beginners. *(3 marks)*

21 (a) When might you use manual guidance in the teaching of skills? *(1 mark)*

(b) List the disadvantages of this approach. *(3 marks)*

Contemporary studies

22 (a) What are the four main concepts behind sport? *(1 mark)*

(b) What are the main features of one of these concepts? *(4 marks)*

23 (a) What is the CCPR? *(1 mark)*

(b) What did 'Sport for All' aim to do? *(1 mark)*

24 Using one emergent country as an example, state which sport has developed there. Give reasons for the development of that sport. *(4 marks)*

25 (a) Define 'egalitarianism'. *(1 mark)*

(b) What happens in reality under this system? *(1 mark)*

(c) How is this socialist model justified by the state? *(1 mark)*

26 What are the driving forces behind the capitalist model? State the impact that each driving force has on the development of sport in multi-party democracies. *(4 marks)*

27 Inequalities exist in PE and sport. Give the disadvantages that may be experienced by one minority group. *(6 marks)*

Questions

Exercise physiology

28 What does ATP stand for in terms of human movement? *(1 mark)*

29 If exercise is to continue for more than 10–12 seconds another method of ATP regeneration must be used.

   (a) What is this system called?

   (b) About how long can exercise be maintained using this system? *(2 marks)*

30 After completing exercise involving this system, why is it important to continue with some form of gentle exercise? *(5 marks)*

31 Define the term 'basal metabolic rate'. *(1 mark)*

32 (a) List the components of health-related fitness. *(4 marks)*

   (b) List the components of skill related fitness. *(5 marks)*

33 (a) What is Maximum VO_2? *(2 marks)*

   (b) What adaptations occur in the body to improve an athlete's Maximum VO_2? *(5 marks)*

34 What do you understand by the term 'the principle of overload'? Illustrate your answer with examples from weight training. *(4 marks)*

35 What do you understand by 'principle of reversibility' in terms of training and fitness? *(3 marks)*

36 What do you understand by the term 'fartlek'? Illustrate your answer with a practical example? *(3 marks)*

37 (a) What short-term changes occur in the body during high-energy exercise? *(5 marks)*

   (b) Outline the main adaptations in the muscular, cardiovascular and respiratory systems that the body produces as a response to long-term training programmes. *(6 marks)*

Biomechanics

38 (a) Define the term 'friction'. *(2 marks)*

   (b) Give two examples from sport where players try to increase friction in order to improve performance. (Exclude examples where interactions with air or water are responsible for the friction force.) *(2 marks)*

   (c) Give two examples from sport where players try to decrease friction in order to improve performance. (Exclude examples where interactions with air or water are responsible for the friction force.) *(2 marks)*

39 *Figure 1* shows four forces acting on a scrummaging machine immediately prior to starting to move across the surface of the pitch.

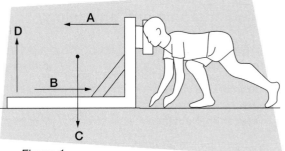

Figure 1

Match the letters A, B, C and D on the diagram with the following forces:

   (a) weight of the scrummaging machine;

   (b) the 'normal' force;

   (c) the friction force;

   (d) the applied force exerted by the player. *(4 marks)*

40 Consider the three diagrams X, Y and Z, in *Figure 2* and for each, state whether it represents a first-, second- or third-class lever system. Explain your choices. *(6 marks)*

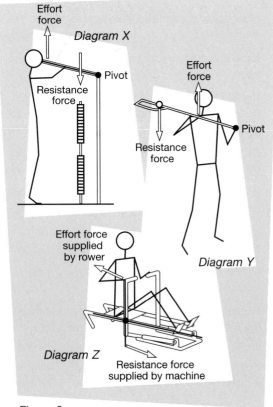

Figure 2

41 State Newton's three Laws of Motion as they can be applied to rational motion. *(6 marks)*

42 Explain what is meant by torque and identify the factors that may be varied to change the magnitude of torque. *(4 marks)*

43 *Figure 3* below shows a diagram of a sportsperson's foot pivoting at a point under the ball of the foot.

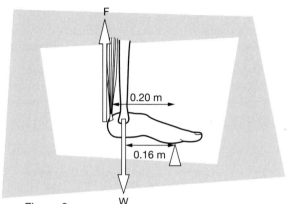

Figure 3

W = Weight of the person which acts vertically through the ankle joint via the tibia: in this case,

W = 700 Newtons.

F = Force of contraction in the gastrocnemeus/soleus muscles which passes through the Achilles tendon as shown.

(a) Use your knowledge of the principle of moments applied to this lever system to calculate force F. Show all your workings.
(4 marks)

(b) Sketch the lever system which would represent the action of the biceps muscle in flexing the arm. *(3 marks)*

(c) Explain why biceps/radius lever system is much less efficient at exerting force on the surroundings than the ankle/calf muscle lever system. *(3 marks)*

44 State Newton's Law of Gravitation. *(3 marks)*

45 *Figure 4* shows three positions of the jumper:

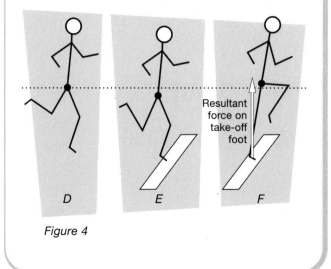

Figure 4

D – two strides away from the take-off board;

E – just before take-off, with take-off foot in contact with the board;

F – at the moment of take-off.

The large dot on the diagrams is the position of her centre of mass and the broken line is a horizontal line through the first position of the centre of mass (position of dot at D).

(a) Explain the meaning of the term 'centre of mass'. *(2 marks)*

(b) Sketch a graph showing the vertical velocity of the centre of mass (y axis) against time (x axis), as the jumper moves from position D through E to position F. *(3 marks)*

(c) Position F shows a resultant force acting on the jumper's take-off foot. Explain the meaning of the term 'resultant'. *(1 mark)*

(d) Use your sketch graph to explain why there must be a resultant vertical force acting on the jumper between E and F. *(4 marks)*

46 Just before take-off, the direction of the resultant force on the athlete's foot *(Figure 4)* passes behind her centre of mass.

(a) What effect does this have on the jumper's body after take-off? *(3 marks)*

(b) What techniques could the jumper use to counteract this effect? *(2 marks)*

(c) Describe the motion of the jumper's centre of mass after take-off but before landing. *(3 marks)*

47 A hockey player strikes a ball.

(a) Sketch a graph of the force applied to the ball (y axis) against time (x axis). *(2 marks)*

(b) Explain how using a follow-through would effect the motion of the struck ball. *(4 marks)*

Psychology

48 Define personality? *(1 mark)*

49 What possible problems can occur when researching a performer's personality? *(4 marks)*

50 What is cognitive dissonance? *(3 marks)*

51 (a) Explain the possible causes of aggression in team sports. *(3 marks)*

(b) How might aggression be prevented from occurring in performers in a team? *(4 marks)*

52 (a) Describe the characteristics of a person showing a NACH personality. *(3 marks)*

(b) Describe the characteristics of a person showing NAF personality. *(3 marks)*

Questions

53 (a) Evaluation apprehension is a powerful influence on performance. Explain the effect it can have during performance.   *(4 marks)*

(b) How might a coach go about helping the athlete to cope with these influences? *(3 marks)*

54 Give three examples of ways to measure stress and highlight the problems associated with each one.   *(6 marks)*

55 The technique of visualization (using imagery) is often used by athletes just before an event. Describe this technique and highlight its advantages and disadvantages.   *(4 marks)*

56 Leadership is an important aspect of optimizing a team's performance. What qualities would you look for in an effective leader?   *(7 marks)*

57 (a) What is the Ringelmann Effect?   *(2 marks)*

(b) What is social loafing?   *(2 marks)*

History

58 Until relatively recently, field sports played an important part in people's lives in this country. Describe the main purposes that hunting served.   *(2 marks)*

59 Describe, for a sport of your choice, how both the rich and the poor became involved.   *(2 marks)*

60 How did public school boys develop games to suit their environment?   *(4 marks)*

61 Why did public school headmasters allow pupils to play games?   *(4 marks)*

62 Why did the growing middle classes want to promote sport for their factory workers?   *(4 marks)*

63 Describe the sporting activities that girls were expected to do in Victorian schools in Britain.   *(2 marks)*

64 Why did the government like the 1902 Model Course and why did educationalists dislike it?   *(6 marks)*

65 How did the role of the PE teacher change between 1904 and 1954? Use examples of subject content during the period to highlight your answer.   *(6 marks)*

66 List the differences between teaching PE and coaching a sport.   *(3 marks)*

67 Who was Madame Bergman-Osterbeg? What influence has she had on the spread of women's sport over the years?   *(3 marks)*

68 (a) Define the term 'amateur'.   *(1 mark)*

(b) Define the term 'professional'.   *(1 mark)*

(c) List two major developments in the rise of the professional sportsperson.   *(2 marks)*

Comparative studies

69 (a) What is the 'American Dream'?   *(1 mark)*

(b) What is the 'win ethic'?   *(1 mark)*

70 How is mass participation in sport encouraged in the USA?   *(4 marks)*

71 (a) How does nationalisation play a part in sports in France? Give five examples. *(5 marks)*

(b) How is compulsory PE and sport assessed in French secondary schools? State the names of the practical tests.   *(3 marks)*

72 What changes were brought in after the poor performances by Australian athletes at the 1976 Olympics?   *(4 marks)*

Answers

> The following answers are not model answers. They provide the basic information that students should have included. The presentation will be individual to students.

Applied anatomy and physiology

1 The alternating bands of light and dark areas in the sarcomere give clues as to how Huxley's sliding filament theory works. When an impulse arrives at the muscle cell, this triggers the release of calcium ions. These calcium ions bind to troponin and cause the binding sites on actin to be exposed. ATP is broken down and energy is released. This energy is used to power the myosin head. The cross-bridges attach, detach and re-attach further along the actin filament – pulling the actin past the myosin. This has the effect of shortening the length of the sarcomere and so shortening the muscle.

2 *Fast twitch fibres* are bigger than slow twitch fibres and have larger motor neurones. This means they can generate force faster. However, fast twitch fibres tire more quickly than slow twitch fibres.

   Slow twitch fibres contract at a rate of about 20% slower than fast twitch fibres. Because they are smaller than fast twitch fibres, slow twitch fibres generate force comparatively slowly.

   Slow twitch fibres do not fatigue as easily as fast twitch fibres, which makes them perfect for low-level activities. Fast twitch fibres tire more quickly, which means they are only useful for high-level activities. The Fast Twitch High Oxidative Glycolytic (FOG) type of fibres are used for longer sprint events; the Fast Twitch Glycolytic (FTG) type are used for shorter sprint events. (FOG have a greater resistance to fatigue than FTG. This is entirely due to endurance training, which encourages muscular adaptation.)

3 (a) A motor unit has a motor neurone controlling large numbers of individual fibres. The axon of the motor neurone – which runs from the spinal cord – branches as it reaches the muscle. The branches connect with a structure called the motor end plate.

   (b) Each muscle fibre is served by a nerve fibre that is attached to the muscle. The nerve impulses that are carried along the nerve fibres are fired in different patterns. The stimulus may activate one motor unit to produce a twitch. Muscles will contract for longer than a fraction of a second when a stimulus occurs that activates many motor neurones.

   (c) The human body increases the size of the force of muscle contraction by wave summation (i.e. by sending impulses one after the other in quick succession). The stimuli arrive so fast there is no time for any relaxation of the muscle. A state of 'absolute contraction' then occurs.

4 (a) The student's heart rate starts at the normal resting rate. There is an increase just before starting the bleep test as adrenaline is released. The rise continues as the test starts. Then there is a steep rise in heart rate as the exercise increases in intensity. A plateau occurs in the heart rate as the bleep test is reaching the higher levels. When the level 12 is reached and the student slows down the heart rate begins to fall. This drop in heart rate slows down in order for the body to clear the by-products of tissue respiration, before finally returning to normal (resting rate).

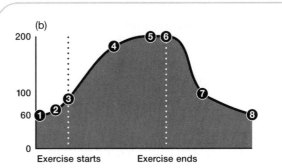

(b)

5 Heart rate x Stroke volume = Cardiac output

6 Training can improve the stroke volume (both the size of the heart and the muscle wall thickness increase), which therefore causes an increase in the cardiac output.

7 The heartbeat is initiated by electrical impulses that originate from the heart's 'pacemaker', the sino-atrial node. The impulse travels down the myocardium of the atrium until it reaches the atrio-ventricular node. A short delay then occurs, to allow atrial systole to complete. The impulse then enters specialist tissues called 'bundles of HIS' which branch through the septum as Purkinje fibres. Thse connect to myocardium fibres that cause the ventricles to contract (ventricular systole). This process can be seen by tracing the electrical signals in the heart using an electrocardiogram (ECG).

8 The 'lub' sound is the heart forcing blood out of the atria into the ventricles. Semi-lunar valves remain closed, but atrio-ventricular valves close after the passage of blood.

   Once the blood has left the heart and the contraction ceases, the semi-lunar valves snap shut – causing the 'dub' sound heard through the stethoscope.

9 The medulla oblongata acts as a relay centre for messages between parts of the brain and the body. It has vital reflex centres that regulate heart beat. Information received from sensors in the cardiac centre of the medulla oblongata is interpreted and redirected via nerves.

10 (a) An artery is surrounded by 'smooth' muscle; a vein has a muscular coat, which affects the tone.

   (b) The 'smooth' muscle of the artery controls the size of the lumen through which the blood flows. The oxygenated blood flows in spurts through the artery as the heart beats.

   The muscular coat of a vein allows changes in capacity of the blood flow. This is important when carrying deoxygenated blood back to the heart.

11 'Minute volume' (MV) is the volume of air you breathe in per minute.

   'Tidal volume' (TV) is the volume of air you breathe in (or out) with each breath.

   'Respiratory rate' (RR) is the number of breaths you take per minute.

12 Keeping the centre of gravity low at the start of the sprint results in more forward momentum. This is because the force from the leg muscles pushing onto the ground and the ground returning that force to the feet enables the sprinter to shift their centre of gravity.

13 Levers have two functions:
   • to apply force (strength) to an object – the longer the lever distance from the force to the fulcrum the greater the force generated;

Answers

- to move a resistance a greater distance or through a greater range of movement.

Also, joints work most efficiently at around a 90° angle of pull.

Using all of this information can help a golfer improve their game. A good swing and a long, heavy club should enable the golfer to hit the ball further.

Acquisition of skills

14 Ability is the quality or skill that you have which makes it possible to do something.

Three possible examples:
- Ability to co-ordinate when dribbling a football.
- Flexibility when doing gymnastics.
- Using muscular power when lifting weights.

15 Using golf as an example, the open loop theory of motor control is as follows:
- The brain sends action commands to the muscles, in one chunk – eye on ball; knees flexed; pull back club; accelerate club to ball and follow through.
- Feedback may be available but it does not control the action.

16 Using catching a cricket ball as an example, the closed loop theory of motor control is as follows:
- The brain makes a decision – catch that ball!
- Some information is sent to initiate muscle action – eye on ball; move into position; hold hands ready; take catch.
- Feedback is available and is used to alter initial movements according to the new needs – the ball has bounced out of hands; keep eyes on ball; move hands to new position; try again.

17 (a) Feedback can provide motivation, especially for a beginner. For example: 'You hit nearly all of your forehands as winners. Well done!'

(b) Feedback can act as a motivator for reinforcement for an experienced player. For example: 'You know you can hit better forehands. You were hitting the ball too late. Let's go and work on that!'

18 'Reaction time' is the time from the first appearance of the stimulus to the initiation of the first movement. For example, the moment a tennis player is aware of the opponent sending the ball over the net to a particular area of the court, a decision being made to hit a forehand and the first movement to that part of the court.

'Movement time' is the time taken for the movement, initiated by the stimulus, to begin and then be completed. For example, in tennis the moment when the receiver begins to move into position to hit a forehand shot, including backswing, until the moment the player comes back (after impact) into a ready position to prepare for the next shot.

'Response time' is the time between the first presentation of stimulus to the movement ending. For example, the tennis player becomes aware of the opponent sending the ball over the net to a particular area of the court, decides to play a forehand, moves into position to hit a forehand shot, lifts the racquet back, swings through the forehand, makes impact, and moves back into a ready position to prepare for the next shot.

19 The three stages or phases of learning:
- Cognitive or Understanding phase
- Associative or Verbal motor phase
- Autonomous or Motor phase

20 A distributed practice style of teaching allows beginners to take rests between practice, in which they can mentally rehearse the skills involved. It is a useful technique when teaching complex skills and for young pupils with short attention spans.

21 (a) You might use manual guidance when teaching:
- someone to swim;
- trampoline techniques;
- rock climbing.

(b) If overused the performer may become dependent on help or may lose motivation as they are a passive learner.

Contemporary studies

22 (a) play; physical recreation; physical education; sport

(b) They might have chosen any of the following:

Play:
- biological – instinctual part of learning process in developing skills
- psychological – learning about self
- sociological – to practice social roles
- children's play – to learn about life
- adults' play – to escape the stresses of everyday life.

Physical recreation:
- relaxation and recuperation
- can require limited organisation
- participant in charge of time and place
- personal goals (e.g. creative, spiritual) and rewards
- mental pleasure, enjoyment, non-productive.

Physical education:
- to impart knowledge and values through physical activities
- structured lessons, usually in an institution
- develops practical skills to be able to participate in activities
- develops social skills, team working, co-operation and leadership... often within lifestyle activities
- extra curricular activities out of formal lesson times
- examinations (GCSE, A-level, degree) raised the profile of PE and encouraged career development
- develops values – social, instrumental, humanistic.

Sport:
- competitive
- highly organised – time and space designated
- formal rules
- requires higher level of skill and commitment
- develop sportsmanship
- intrinsic rewards (own achievement, satisfaction)
- extrinsic rewards (cups, money, titles, etc.)
- the 'letter' of playing the game – by the rules
- the 'spirit' of playing the game – fair play, high morals.

23 (a) The Central Council for Physical Recreation

(b) 'Sport for All' aimed to increase participation by all regardless of sex, age, race or class.

24 Students might choose any emergent country, but it's likely they will select one of the following:

Indonesia – badminton
- Minority sport which suits country
- Olympic sport – thus seen by the world
- Easy to administer
- Non-contact – non-aggressive
- Small-sided game – small population
- Requires small physique, dexterity and quick reactions
- Little equipment or space needed
- Slow pace – and ideal for playing in the tropics.

The Caribbean – cricket
- Traditional and established game
- Brought islands and people together in common purpose
- Team game – co-operation

- Outdoor game – healthy
- Commonwealth sport – able to play other nations
- International reputation
- Income to islands.

Kenya – middle and long distance running
- Olympic sport – high profile
- Suited to lifestyle – used to running long distances
- Little expense or technical knowledge needed
- Good training at altitude
- A few athletes can create great national pride.

25 (a) Egalitarianism is the belief that all people are equal and should have the same rights and opportunities.

(b) In reality, often the talented are given privileges at the expense of the ordinary person.

(c) This is justified by the state to achieve role models for international exposure to promote the country's status.

26 Nationalism – sport is used as a symbol of national identity and a vehicle to promote it.

Excellence – sport is an arena where individuals can achieve optimum potential, seen through their own performance or the commercial value.

Recreational – sports are an escape from work and duty.

Commercial – sport is seen as a commodity and if the commodity is scarce it becomes valuable.

27 They are asked to give the disadvantages for *one* group. They could pick any of the following:

Race
Opportunity:
- Parental expectations
- Non-acceptance in clubs may be a barrier
- May be affected by religious beliefs (e.g. muslim girls)
- Lack of finance means little choice (many low paid)
- Cultures may not rate PE/sport highly
- 'staking' – assumption that you play in a particular position in the team
- lack of career opportunities – majority of coaches are white

Provision:
- associated with a particular sport (e.g. Asians playing cricket)...therefore little provision in other sports
- lack of single sex lessons
- lack of changing facilities to cater for religious restrictions
- information not easily available
- coaches not available

Esteem:
- Lack of role models to give hope to achieve
- Poorly paid jobs add to low self-esteem
- Media coverage of indigenous sports is low

Disability
Opportunity:
- Some sports may not cater for disability – therefore restricted choice
- Few disabled sports clubs and restricted membership to others
- Few coaches so poor prospects
- Fewer opportunities to achieve excellence

Provision:
- Lack of specialist equipment
- Poor wheelchair access to leisure centres and swimming pools
- Inadequate changing facilities
- Transport to activities may not be possible
- Cost of special provision may be prohibitive

Esteem:
- Perceived to be not able to achieve and the

assumption that they cannot do sport – a myth and stereotype
- Few role models – paraplegic games and marathons only beginning to be given media coverage
- Assumed lack of knowledge
- Perceived as not interesting or exciting enough ...therefore not taken seriously.

Gender
Opportunity:
- Looking after family – less leisure time
- certain religious restrictions
- fewer female coaches, managers and administrators therefore limited career opportunities
- some clubs have membership restrictions – although law is changing
- lack of competition opportunity
- restricted choice of activities and those choices may favour males
- considered incapable and not aggressive enough

Provision:
- lack of creche facilities
- few females on governing bodies and little input in decision making
- few female coaches
- lower pay and prize money
- may lack money to spend on sport if not working
- lack of transport
- competitions may be restricted to single sex
- clubs may restrict playing times or provide inferior changing facilities

Esteem:
- think they can't do sport – poor self-image
- lack of many role models
- media coverage poor
- lack of sponsorship
- not taken seriously by spectators
- affected by myths

Age
Opportunity:
- young – too early with hard training can 'burn out'
- young – reliant on parental attitude and finances
- participation of 50+ age group restricted, few veterans' clubs and teams
- age restrictions in some clubs
- curriculum and extra curricular opportunities dependent on schools – relies on PE staff enthusiasm

Provision:
- facilities dependant on geographical location
- few activity sessions specifically for older people or teenagers
- transport may be reliant on goodwill of family and friends
- fees may be prohibitive

Esteem:
- media coverage minimal for elderly and very young
- few role models
- elderly perceived as only involved for recreation
- peer pressure can affect youngsters' perception of sport, particularly girls

Class
Opportunity:
- 'working class' – little leisure time, lack of finance, difficult to work and compete at a high level
- restricted access to certain clubs
- 'middle class' – more leisure time and wealth to choose activities

Provision:
- 'working class' may experience limited facilities and coaches – reliant on sponsorship for funding

Answers

- wealthy individuals have the ability to pay a coach, buy equipment and clothing and to travel to training and competition

  Esteem:
  - role models can give hope to those from deprived backgrounds – seen as way out and means to achieve wealth
  - Media can help promote and gain sponsorship
  - Less wealthy could be seen as less able or knowledgeable

Exercise physiology

28 Adenosine triphosphate – the main supplier of metabolic energy in all living cells.

29 (a) Lactic acid system, or glycolysis.

(b) Exercise can be sustained using this system for between 30 seconds and 1 minute.

30 Gentle exercise, or warm-down, after training involving the lactic acid system is important as this maintains higher respiration rate and flushes lactic acid out of fast twitch fibres.

31 Basal metabolic rate (BMR) is the energy you need just to be alive, awake and comfortably warm.

32 (a) Health-related fitness components:
- aerobic capacity
- strength
- flexibility
- body composition

(b) Skill-related fitness components:
- speed
- reaction time
- agility
- balance
- coordination

33 (a) VO_2 max. is the amount of energy used during maximal exercise. It is directly related to the amount of oxygen consumed.

VO_2 – v = volume per minute; O_2 = oxygen

An athlete's VO_2 max. is determined by the efficiency of their cardiac system, respiratory system, and other physiological characteristics (e.g. muscle fibre types).

(b) The following adaptations occur in the body to improve an athlete's VO_2 max.:
- increased capillarisation
- increase in red blood cells
- increased cardiac output
- increased myoglobin content
- increase in size and number of mitochondria by up to 20%.

34 The human body is designed to adapt to new demands made on it. So if we put the body under more strain, it will respond by changing to meet the new demands. Overload is achieved either by:
- Increasing the number of times the weight lifter trained
- Increasing the amount of work the weight lifter does in training
- Increasing the length of time the weight lifter trains.

35 The body must 'work' to remove the changes that occur during exercise (increase in levels of carbon dioxide and lactic acid; decreases in levels of phosphocreatine, glycogen, triglyceride and oxygen/myoglobin). There is a cost in energy to do this. The body does not immediately return to resting levels of heart rate or breathing rate. This increased aerobic respiration rate is used to repay the oxygen debt.

36 Fartlek is a form of aerobic training. It is based on changes of speed. For example, 5 minutes of gentle jogging; then 5 minutes of fast walk; then 50-metre sprints every 200 metres; then uphill jog with 10 fast strides every minute; and so on.

37 (a) **Heart:**
Exercise changes the chemical balance of the body:
- lactic acid increases
- $CO_2 + O_2$ levels change
- and temperature increases.

  This produces stimuli for the cardiac control centre to respond to.

  Nerves: the sympathetic nerve controlling the sino-atrial node (pacemaker) is stimulated to increase heart rate.

  Chemical: adrenaline is released in the blood, increasing the heart rate even before exercise.

  Cardiac output increases because the heart rate increases; and venous return increases which in turn increases the amount of blood entering the heart. More blood in the heart and stronger more frequent contractions leads to increased cardiac output.

  Lungs:
  - Changes to the relative proportions of CO_2 and O_2 are detected in the respiratory centre, which responds by increasing minute ventilation.
  - Minute ventilation is a function of the number of breath and the tidal volume. Tidal volume increases by drawing upon the spare lung capacity, known as inspiratory reserve volume and expiratory reserve volume.
  - The respiratory muscles, intercostals, diaphragm and scaleni become more active, especially on expiration. This increases the volume of the thoracic cavity and decreases it with greater force.

  Blood:
  - Blood changes its constitution during exercise. This carries the messages that are detected by receptors to initiate changes in HR and ventilation.
  - Blood becomes thicker during intense activity as plasma volume decreases due to sweating.
  - Glucose levels begin to drop.
  - Blood acidity increases due to lactic acid. This may, if not controlled, lead to a detrimental effect on muscle activity.
  - Oxygen concentrations drop dramatically, thus increasing diffusion at the lungs.
  - Blood pressure increases as cardiac output increases.
  - Blood flow speeds up.
  - More blood is directed to the muscles and away from other areas. Vasodilation in arteries to muscles and in muscle capillaries aids blood flow here.
  - Vasoconstriction around non-essential areas decreases blood flow in these areas.

  Muscles:
  - Increases in the intensity and frequency of contractions lead to a greater use of energy, thus increasing cell respiration. These changes stimulate the rest of the body to adapt.
  - The body's fuel energy stores of phosphocreatine, glycogen and triglycerides are gradually depleted.
  - The myoglobin in the muscles gives up its oxygen stores for cell respiration. Thus oxygen is diffused more quickly as the partial pressure difference between cell and capillary is greater.
  - Carbon dioxide and lactic acid levels increase in the muscles and need to be removed by the blood.
  - The energy conversion in the muscle is notoriously inefficient. It is only between 14%–25% efficient, with most energy being released as heat, thus increasing body temperature.

  (b) **Muscular:**
  - Muscles grow larger and stronger through exercise.

- Myoglobin concentration increases.
- Mitochondria becomes more numerous.
- Enzymes work much more efficiently allowing greater cell respiration.
- Muscles store larger amounts of glycogen and triglycerides.

Cardiovascular:
- The muscles of the heart wall (myocardium) grow in size and strength after regular exercise. This allows the heart to contract with more force, therefore ejecting more blood per heart beat.
- Increased heart size means increased stroke volume. Therefore at rest the athlete's heart has to pump less times to move the same amount of blood as an untrained heart. This results in lower resting heart rate (bradycardia).
- At maximum levels of effort, stroke volume is increased and heart rate is high. Thus more oxygen is delivered to the working muscles, increasing efficiency and increasing VO_2 max.
- The volume of blood increases, due mostly to increased plasma levels. More red blood cells are also created, allowing greater oxygen-carrying capacity.
- Acidity of the blood decreases at low level exercise as their aerobic system is more efficient.
- At maximal levels of exercise, blood acidity is higher in athletes as they have a greater tolerance of its effects.
- Arterial walls become more elastic with endurance training, allowing tolerance of changes in blood pressure. There is greater capillarisation in the lungs and muscles allowing greater diffusion of oxygen.

Respiratory:
- Maximum minute volume is increased.
- The respiratory muscles are stronger and more efficient, making respiration easier.
- Lung capacity improves as training increases. Capillarisation around the alveoli allows greater areas of lung to be utilized.
- Enzymes work much more efficiently allowing greater cell respiration.
- Muscles store larger amounts of glycogen and triglycerides.

Biomechanics

38 (a) Friction is the force that acts between two surfaces to oppose motion.
    (b) Studded boots in football; the use of magnesium carbonate in gymnastics to aid grip on high bar.
    (c) Waxing skis to aid sliding movement; brushing ice in curling to aid sliding movement.

39 (a) C; (b) D; (c) B; (d) A

40 X: second class as the pivot is at one end of the rigid bar with the resistance in the middle and effort at the other end. (Load arm < effort arm)
    Y: third class as the pivot is at one end, effort in middle and resistance at the other end. (Load arm > effort arm)
    Z: first class as the pivot is in the middle of effort and resistance.

41 First Law of Motion: a body will remain at rest or rotate with uniform angular velocity unless an external torque is applied to it.
    Second Law of Motion: angular acceleration is proportional to the torque applied and acts in the direction of the torque.
    Third Law of Motion: for every torque applied by a body there is an equal and opposite torque applied to the body.

42 Torque is the 'turning effect' of a force. Factors affecting magnitude include force applied and perpendicular distance of the line of action at point of entry:
    $W = \frac{78}{14} = 5.57$ rad/sec

43 (a) Taking anti-clockwise moments as positive.
    W x 0.16 – F x 0.20 = 0
    W = 700 N
    700 x 0.16 – 0.20 F = 0
    112 = 0.2 F
    F = 560 N
    (b)
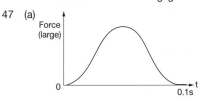
    (c) The biceps/radius lever system is less efficient than the ankle/calf muscle lever system as the biceps lever always has a larger load arm compared with effort arm (i.e. perpendicular distance of load to pivot is greater than perpendicular distance of effort to pivot).

44 Any two bodies attract each other with a force proportional to the product of their masses and universally proportional to the square of the distance between them.

45 (a) A single point that represents the concentration of the body's mass.
    (b)
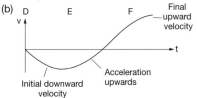
    (c) The resultant is the overall/sum vector of all the forces acting.
    (d) The upward slope between E and F means upward acceleration. With F = Ma, this means a net (resultant) upward force as Force is proportional to Acceleration.

46 (a) Resultant causes torque about C of M, causing a clockwise rotation of the body; tends to make her fall forwards on her face.
    (b) Counteract with arms
        Hitch kick
        Hang
    (c) Parabola
        Gravity is predominant force acting
        Air resistance effect is negligible

47 (a)
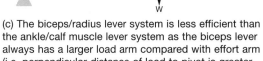
    (b) Extends the time over which force acts; which increases the impulse and momentum of the ball. Velocity of ball increased and degree of control/direction improved.

48 Personality is *either* 'The sum total of an individual's characteristics which makes him or her unique' *or* 'The overall pattern of psychological characteristics that makes each person unique'.

49 There are problems in ensuring validity and reliability. All techniques may be time consuming and costly. The interpretation of results may cause over-generalization, particularly if small numbers are used.

50 Cognitive dissonance is a mismatch in the Triadic Model. This causes an imbalance in the mind of the person being persuaded. You must act to reduce this

Answers

imbalance by changing behaviour to meet new criteria, based on new information.

51 (a) Possible causes:
- natural instinct – cultural background often disproves this and aggression is often not spontaneous
- frustration – a person is blocked, they are frustrated and release the tension through aggressive action
- social learning – people see others being aggressive and imitate this behaviour.

(b) Combatting aggression:
- Control of arousal levels (stress management)
- Avoidance of situations that cause aggression
- Stopping aggressive players from further participation
- Rewarding 'turning the other cheek'
- Showing non-aggressive role models
- Punishing aggression
- Reinforcement of non-aggression (largely by significant others)
- Handling responsibility to an aggressive player.

52 (a) NACH personality:
- determined to see a task through
- work quickly at a task
- take risks
- enjoy a challenge
- take responsibility
- like to know how they have been judged.

(b) NAF personality:
- easily persuaded from taking the challenge
- work at tasks slowly or not at all
- avoid situations where they or their ego is put at risk
- avoid responsibility
- prefer not to be judged and do not want to know how they have been judged.

53 (a) Evaluation apprehension creates increased arousal levels, especially if the audience is made up of significant others for the performer.

(b) A coach might try:
- using relaxation techniques
- using mental imagery to block out audience
- teaching new skills in a non-evaluative way
- explaining to athletes how audiences are likely to affect them
- encouraging a supportive atmosphere amongst team members.

54 Self report questionnaires – may not always give a truthful picture.

Physiological measurements – often require bulky, expensive equipment and some of the measurements can be affected by exercise, before or afterwards.

Behavioural observation – needs to be studied over an extended period, before, during and after training and competition.

55 Visualization (imagery) is the creation of a mental picture to relax or prepare the athlete for activity. It comes in two forms:
- External – watching yourself perform, from outside your body
- Internal – seeing your performance from your body.

Imagery for relaxation often takes the athlete to comfortable surroundings (e.g. a favourite place, a tropical island). Visualization often involves mental rehearsal of the skills to be attempted.

56 Leadership qualities:
- Ability to communicate
- Enthusiasm
- High motivation
- A vision of what need to be done
- High ability
- Inspirational qualities – charisma.

57 (a) The Ringelmann effect – experiments have shown that teams of eight (say, tug-of-war) do not work eight times better than eight individuals; some team members lose their motivation in a team.

(b) Social loafing – team players lose motivation as they feel their contribution is not visible and therefore not valued.

History

58 Hunting served two main purposes – food and recreation. For the poor, hunting for food was a necessity, to feed the family. They were either involved in employment to feed the wealthy or in poaching (stealing animals from other people's property). The wealthy, on the other hand, often hunted for leisure. This allowed them to show off their athleticism, to challenge themselves physically and to enjoy a social occasion.

59 The answer will depend on the sport chosen by the student. The following are possible answers:

Cricket
- Cricket was enjoyed by all sections of society. It could be played on the rough village wicket with a minimum of equipment, or in the fine setting of a country property.
- The gentry could play in the same team as the working class, but both sections had clearly defined roles. The former dictated tactics, the latter chased after the ball.

Tennis
- The servants of the wealthy saw this game and derived their own version. This was often played in the courtyards of local pubs. This was convenient as it provided both competitors and spectators.

Mob football
- It was a game played by the lower classes and despised by the wealthy. The wealthy were worried that their property would be destroyed by the violent games.

60 • Games changed to suit available playing space.
- Different sports played at different times of the year to suit conditions.
- Rules were developed.
- Inter-house competitions allowed the sport to become regular and competitive.

61 Games:
- encouraged their moral development
- developed leadership
- developed courage
- pupils learnt to put team before self
- usefully occupied free time.

62 For factory workers sport:
- meaningfully occupied free time
- improved health
- boosted morale
- created worker loyalty
- showed the benefits that they themselves had gained from participating while at school.

63 In ladies' academies they taught dancing, a form of callisthenics, sewing, singing, playing the piano, verse speaking, posture and any other graces it was felt important for a woman to have.

By the 1880s tennis and cricket were being played in girls' schools. The girls wore their normal clothing to be worn and the games did not involve contact.

64 The 1902 Model course:

Government:
- disciplined
- created young soldiers
- promoted health

- provided a scapegoat for recent failures in the Boer War.
  Educationalists:
- treated children as adults
- limited educational value
- no differentiation between girls and boys.

65 Role of the PE teacher:
- Developed from a trainer who taught exercise-related drill to an educationalist who taught skills, games and gymnastics.
- The teaching style moved from being autocratic where there was a one-way flow of commands (e.g. 'attention', 'about turn') to a mixed style that varied from autocratic to self-discovery lesson whose content was more varied.
- Initially the process was more important than the pupils. This changed and the needs of pupils were taken into consideration. Enjoyment, skill development and social development became more important than just obedience.

66 PE teaching
- time is spent on general exercise
- participants are there because it is part of the curriculum
- groups are of mixed ability.
  Sports coaching
- more time is spent on an activity
- the participants are usually there by choice
- groups being coached are often of a similar ability.

67 • Madame Bergman-Osterbeg was involved with PE in London and among other achievements introduced a ladies PE College in 1895. This influenced the spread of women's sport.
- Some of her former pupils set up their own colleges, thereby encouraging more female PE teachers to enter the profession.
- Madame Bergman-Osterbeg's philosophy was based around a mixture of Swedish gymnastics and team games. She advocated single sex lessons.

68 (a) 'Amateur' means taking part in sport for enjoyment and not getting paid or receiving prize money.
   (b) 'Professional' means being paid (some highly!) to take part on sport – playing, coaching or managing.
   (c) Any two from the following:
- The modern Olympic Games began in 1896, with the intention that amateurs would compete against one another. There would be no prize money for the winners, only medals.
- As sports developed there was more scope for professionalism. To be a good player you needed to devote time and money to training. You needed money to attract the best players to your team in order that you could do well in the leagues and attract supporters.
- As the class system was gradually eroded, the stigmatism of being a professional diminished.
- The abolition of the maximum wage meant players could negotiate wages and this turned them from tradesmen into professionals.
- In soccer the maximum wage for any player in England was £4 in 1900. George Eastham, of Newcastle United, went on strike in 1961 over the maximum wage (£10 a week then). A couple of years later, Johnny Haynes of Fulham became the first £100-a-week soccer player.

Comparative studies

69 (a) The 'American Dream' is the 'rags to riches' story. It is the idea that everyone and anyone can achieve success/the pursuit of happiness. Sport is seen as a way out of the gutter (e.g. boxing).
   (b) The 'win ethic' means winning is the only thing. This is also known as the Lombardian philosophy, after Vince Lombardi, Head Coach of Green Bay Packers in 1959, who transformed them from a losing baseball team into a major power in the sport. The emphasis is on competition and rewards.

70 Mass participation:
- No specific plans by the federal government.
- Programmes for adults are part of school programmes.
- For children, 'little league sport' (e.g. little league basketball) – originally set up by parents, now a business organisation catering for 8–18 year olds (senior division 13–15; big league 16–18). Attracts media coverage.
- National senior sports organisation – image of a healthy old age.
- No real private sports clubs except elitist ones (tennis and golf). Expensive. Less wealthy involved with activities at:
  – ice rinks
  – swimming pools
  – basketball courts.
- All interested in going to the game (baseball).

71 (a) Nationalism:
- In the post-war period President de Gaulle reinforced a feeling of nationalism.
- 'Every Frenchman is born a soldier' – feeling of being French is important.
- Rural simplicity and 'taste' – whether it be food, wine or theatre.
- Retention of their language (keen to eliminate English words).
- Intellect important – academic study is a priority (therefore PE is poorly rated in schools).
- Baccalaureate system in upper schools.
- The French enjoy a spectacle (e.g. Tour de France).
- They let themselves go and appreciate the diversity of the countryside.
- Love a test of manliness.
- In sport, play with flair (e.g. World Cup soccer and rugby).
- The French consider the way you win is as important as winning (Olympism).
   (b) 'Le Program' – syllabus for teachers.
   'Le gym' PE is formally assessed with practical tests at:
   15 – *Brevet de Colleges*
   17 – *Brevet d'Enseignement Professionel*
   18 – *Baccalaureate*.

72 Poor performances in the 1976 Olympics led to changes:
- ASC (Australian Sports Commission) researched in other countries to look for most effective method to select and train athletes. Set up the AIS (Australian Institute of Sport), an academy of sport in Canberra (where federal government and ASC located). Realised need for more than one institute of excellence.
- Set up more in other states – Queensland (at Brisbane); Western Australia (at Perth); South Australia (at Adelaide); Victoria (at Melbourne); New South Wales (at Sydney) – each specialised in one sport (e.g. cricket at Adelaide; rugby at Brisbane).
- Now each state devolved with centres of excellence in their main city. All part of AIS federal system. Have programme of talent identification – Sportsleap, Sports search – run at all levels (to identify talent).
- Aussie able – provision for disabled athletes – some sports schools.

Index